Hello Beautiful

Yes, you.

BREAK FREE FROM THE CHAINS OF
REGRET, COMPARISON AND
SELF DOUBT AND

discover the freedom, power and beauty

OF BEING THE REAL YOU

Keryl Pesce

little pink press

Dedication

This book is dedicated to
the most beautiful woman I know . . . my mother.
For never interfering but always supporting.
For being my biggest fan and "groupie."
This book and everything in it is ultimately
a product of you and your love.

I love you.

The Power of a Woman

The power of a woman is born of the most powerful force in the universe . . . the power of love. As she comes to understand this, her every thought, word, and action attract support, guidance and opportunity beyond her wildest imagination. She doesn't look to exert power over others but uses her power in support of others. She doesn't compete, as she knows we make more waves when we come together.

She's not out to change herself. She is out to become herself, fully, completely and clear in her purpose. She appreciates the value of her past and understands all she has experienced didn't happen to her. It happened for her. She arms herself with the lessons she's learned, the gifts she's received and the enormous strength of appreciation for what is while setting her sights on what will be. Her wish isn't to be different. Her wish is to see the glory of who she already is and have the courage to show up every day, in each moment, whole and complete, reaching for the stars while standing firmly on her own two feet.

In seeing the best in others, she realizes the best in herself. And in this knowing, this understanding of the fundamental truth of all life and her eternal connection to it, she organizes the forces of good with every breath she takes, thought she thinks and action she chooses.

She has the power to call forth miracles, for she is one herself.

Contents

Acknowledgements

With deepest gratitude to:

My amazing husband Craig, for keeping your promise and loving me through my darkest time. For all you do to support me and how hard you work so I can do what I do. I love life with you. I love you most.

My beautiful sisters Kim and Karen, through spats, pranks, and occasional skinned knees, we survived and still love each other. We didn't have a lot of money, but we always had love. No matter what life brings us, we will always have each other's backs. I love you both.

Lisa and Dawn Marie, for a lifetime of love, friendship, and laughs. You are the two easiest people in the world to be myself with. What a gift true friendship is.

Jonna Spilbor, for being by my side for silliness and seriousness. I am grateful I've gotten to know how beautiful you are beneath the beauty we see.

Amy Gopel, for loving me when I needed it most.

Jeanne Kelly, for always looking out for me and being my angel here on earth.

Deborah Hanlon, for connecting me with my dad and telling me to "Just write." You helped me open up.

Dave Allis, for helping remove a few burdens to make room in my life and heart to write this.

Introduction

In a world that will tell you ten thousand times a day
you are wrong, I will unflinchingly remind you,
in a thousand different ways, of your rightness.

-LiYana Silver

Hello Beautiful. I am so glad you are here, together with me, and that in the pages ahead, you might find a bit of insight to help you regain what you may have lost . . . yourself, or maybe pieces or parts. Maybe lost isn't even the right word, because you're never too far gone, and you're never less than whole. It's more like helping you rediscover what you haven't been able to see. That's why I'm here. To help you see yourself, all aspects of you and the sum of your experiences, in their completeness . . . and the beauty there is in doing so. Despite what you may currently believe, the sum of you is far more powerful, brilliant, and beautiful than you can imagine . . . including that which you may currently view as flawed or inadequate. I know it's difficult to accept. For now, I am asking for you to trust me . . . at least enough to keep reading.

Allow me to introduce myself. My name is Keryl. I like Neil Diamond, Harry Potter, and doing jigsaw puzzles. I could live in blue jeans and graphic tees. Truth be told, most days I do. I deliberately purchase pink poo bags for my dog because, well, I love pink. And I love my dog. Which is why I allow her to drink out of my water glass. Judge if you will. I'm okay with it. Sometimes I can't see the pickle jar at eye level right in front of me in the refrigerator. Just ask my husband, who will offer the very specific and helpful guidance of "It's right there." But he's great, and I love him too, so he gets a pass . . . most days. I like doing laundry, and I love the sound of my dishwasher running . . . especially in the morning. I can change out a toilet or a light fixture if I need to. My ex had an affair that once brought me to my literal and figurative knees. It turned out to be a gift. I often screw up lyrics to songs. Don't even ask what I thought Bruno Mars put in his cup. I can't remember what I ate for dinner last night, I can't sell to save my life, but I can write and deliver a speech to a thousand people that will bring most to tears. Oh, and I curse.

How's that for a profile? Aren't you glad you bought this book? I believe you will be by the time you're finished because what I've just done is what I want for you . . . to find the courage to show up whole and experience how wonderfully liberating that can be. There was a period of time (five-plus years) that I hid, disliked, and disowned aspects of myself. How'd that work out? I experienced depression, almost constant anxiety, and dangerously low levels of self-worth.

For far too long, my life was dominated by fear, worry, and a deep and penetrating sense of not being enough. Today, these thoughts pop in for a visit now and then, but my life is now dominated with feelings of inner peace, faith in myself and life, and a positive outlook for the future. This is what I want for you as well.

In the pages ahead, you will discover new under-standings, ways of seeing yourself and your life, and choices available to you that will help you experience the amazing freedom and happiness that come from, well, coming together. All of you.

As you find your way through this book and your life going forward, I don't want you to worry about how to be strong, or even if you are capable of being strong enough to recover, get through or handle what life has given or will give you. I'm telling you right here and now, you need not concern yourself with being strong. And here is why. Your job, if we call it that, is to focus on healing, on caring for your tender, vulnerable spots, cleaning them up, giving them the natural time they need to heal, and doing so with the same care and love you would to a cut on a child's finger. Nature heals you all on her own when you set the stage for that to happen. Your emotional wounds respond in much the same way. Here's the best part. Just like scars that form over cuts or burns once you've healed, these previously vulnerable places become your toughest. You are stronger not in spite of your pain, but because of it.

Who you thought you were or your life as you knew it may have been smashed to pieces. But here's the thing. The pieces are all still there. They may scatter, and they may hide. But they don't go away. What each of us has the ability to do is courageously look for and gather the pieces and then reassemble them. The amazing thing is, they will fit together differently, creating a new picture of you and your life, one that shows the world what you are truly made of.

You may be wondering how I know this, how I can be so sure. I'll tell you. Had a psychic told me two years ago that I would write a book about confidence and power, I would have laughed my ass off, called her a fraud, and promptly demanded my money back. I may even have flicked her on the forehead before I spun on my heel and high-tailed it back to the truth. I, yours truly, author of this book, was a full-on hot mess. At that time, the only book I could conceive of writing would have been *How to Fail at Life – 7 Ways Til Sunday on How to Feel Like Shit About Yourself, Doubt Your Abilities and Worth, and Accomplish Nothing*. But I didn't write it, because nobody wants that. Nobody wanted to be like me. *I* didn't even want to be like me.

So believe me, if there is a quiet, subtle voice or maybe even a screaming banshee inside of you that is telling you there is more to you and more to this life than who and what currently shows up, well, take a deep breath, exhale a bit of that doubt and keep reading. There is.

For much of my life, I've been a positive person. It's my conditioned response to look at the bright side, much like a reflex. Tap my knee with what's wrong, and I'll kick you with what's right. It's an attribute people in my life appreciate . . .

some of them. Others, I'm sure, find it a bit annoying. A few have even accused me of living in a place they affectionately call Keryl's Big Bubble World. Whatever. I'm proud of my outlook. In fact, it's more than an attribute to me. It's my identity. Keryl Pesce, always upbeat, always looking at the bright side. Yup. That's me.

I even built a professional life around this identity. Through writing, speaking, the radio show I co-host called Happy Hour, and even the wine brand I co-founded, Happy Bitch Wines, everything I did revolved around happiness. I have obsessively studied the fields of human behavior, happiness, and the law of attraction for more than a decade. The storehouse of knowledge in me as to what makes us tick and what we need to live a happy life is immense. Come to me with something that troubles you, and I guarantee I will have a piece of insight that will help you feel better and see more clearly what empowered action to take next.

So you can imagine my surprise when I found myself falling ass-first down a rabbit hole of fear and doubt. Of what? Pretty much everything . . . my abilities, my worth . . . basically life.

I dreaded running into people I hadn't seen in a while. Inevitably, he or she asked the seemingly normal and innocuous question "So what have you been up to?" But I hated it, because I knew I was about to lie. If I had the balls to answer honestly, I would have said "Oh, just trying everything I can to feel like enough. I've completely lost my confidence. I second guess my every thought and move, which is why I can't accomplish anything. I vaguely remember a time when I felt I belonged in my life and in my skin.

And you?"

My mother raised me to be honest, but my truth was simply too painful and embarrassing. So I lied. I made up something that sounded as if it took a lot of time and quickly turned the conversation around to the other person, hoping my face hadn't gone 50 shades of red.

It felt as if this undercurrent of fear and doubt didn't even belong to me. It felt like I caught a bug, as if by some dumb-ass-luck, I grabbed the door handle at Starbucks, a germ latched on and settled in for a long winter's nap with my body as the cave. Except it didn't last a season. It lasted years. What became painfully obvious was the more I learned about happiness, the worse I felt. Talk about a mind fuck.

It's one thing when something doesn't go as planned, or we get screwed over by someone (Been there. Read *Happy Bitch*.) or are the victim of dumb or bad luck, all of which, admittedly suck. But this was worse. Why? You ask. Two reasons.

One, there ain't a worse battle in the world you'll ever fight than the one that takes place inside you.

You're nodding.

And two, the most challenging hits we take are when a person, event, or experience puts your very *identity* in question, or in my case, completely obliterates it. How do you recover from that? How do you get to a place that you now wonder even exists? The me I thought I was, this world I created, these beliefs I held about happiness, were they even real? My belief system, world, and identity were crumbling.

As I plunged farther into the dark abyss, my bubble floating up, up and away until completely out of sight, I wondered if I'd ever find my way back. The look of pity on Alice's face as I passed her said it all. I think I even heard her mumble "You're screwed," but I'm not sure, so I don't want to say for certain.

I was lost. And I mean big time.

Excuse me, Alice . . . can you tell me how to get to . . . never mind.

Even if I did have the strength to climb out, I hadn't a clue which way was up.

There will be more than a few people close to me who will be surprised when they read this. I hid my insecurities pretty well. I am supposed to be positive. It's who I am. If I talk about what I'm *really* feeling, I'm focusing on the negative. So I didn't. I kicked and shoved it deeper into the already overstuffed and cluttered closet of shame and doubt.

But it didn't help. Not only did it not help, it made matters worse, because the rift between the me on the outside and the me on the inside grew. My denial of my true feelings, my belief that I should hide what I really felt, only intensified my internal conflict.

It's a funny thing we do when we hide our flaws or at least our perception of what we consider flaws. I wrongly believed keeping my secret safe kept me safe. Nothing could have been farther from the truth. Keeping my struggle to myself involved grave risk. My life was on the line, as I danced with the devil herself. Standing at the edge of despair, I questioned the very worth of my life and wondered if no life was a better alternative to the enormous pressure, confusion, and sense of complete failure.

You know the definition of insanity, right? Keep doing

the same thing over and over, expecting a different result. Keep hiding, keep smiling, and it will get better. Except it didn't, and if I wasn't insane, I was certainly well on my way.

I'd like to say a piece of courage showed up one afternoon, but I don't really know if that's what it was. I think it was more like rock bottom with nothing to lose. As I lay in bed in the middle of the day crying, I did something I had never done and that I feared immensely. I reached out and shared my secret, revealed the inside me to the outside world. I texted a friend exactly this: *How can I know as much as I do and still feel this inadequate?*

Backing up my claim as to the version of me I presented to others, she replied "Are you fucking with me, Pesce?" It was inconceivable to her that I could possibly feel inadequate.

"I'm in bed crying," I shared.

What happened next slapped my inner critic, the devil herself, so hard that it's left a mark to this day.

"I love you, Keryl Pesce," she wrote.

My inner critic was, at least for the moment, at a loss for words. She'd been caught in a lie . . . a big, fat, dirty, mean lie. She'd been telling me all along I needed to hide what I was really feeling or people would judge me, not respect me, and not want to be around me.

"What do you have to say to that, bitch?"

Crickets.

"That's what I thought."

My friend continued. "Why do we hide like this? Why are we afraid to show our struggles? We all deal with it. Anyone who says otherwise is lying."

And after a long pause, this, "And we're doing each

other a disservice by hiding it."

Hmmm, so you're telling me you still love me when I'm not a happy person, AND I should talk about this? WTF?

To anyone going through a significant challenge who has asked my advice, I say two things. One, you may not get to choose whether or not to go through this, but you get to choose *how* you go through it. That part is always up to you. Two, find a way to bring meaning to your suffering by responding in such a way you grow and it benefits other people.

I really need to learn to shut my mouth sometimes. The tables turned. Now I needed to take my own advice.

Something shifted in me that day. I'd like to tell you I found one piece of insight, kissed my inner boo-boos, and from there on out, life was good. That's not exactly how it went. But I will tell you my experience that day was a major pivot point. It was a shift in perspective, an "Aha!" moment, a challenge to a firmly-held belief that subsequently led me down a powerful path of discovery and liberation from the self-inflicted chains around my sense of self. I learned more about myself, why I felt the way I did, and most important, what to *do* about it in the months that followed that experience than I learned in a decade of intensive study of self-improvement. What a beautiful gift good friends are.

My girlfriend was right. We are doing ourselves and each other a great disservice by not showing up as our whole selves, by holding back or hiding parts of us, and only showing that which we think will serve or protect us or help us be accepted by others. Doing so creates internal conflict and weakens us. It also prevents us from truly connecting with each other and getting the support we need. Yes, I believe in cultivating a positive mindset, but not at the expense of denying other valid parts of you or your life. A whole version, including those aspects that we perceive as negative, is by far, a stronger and more powerful version, than any masked, filtered, or partial one.

This book is part of my journey to become whole again . . . by showing up as my full and complete self in my life and to you in the pages of this book. We can heal ourselves when we find a way to bring meaning to our suffering. My hope is that you will see we are deeper than the cars we drive, the pictures we post, and the letters before or after our names.

It will do us all a world of good to judge others less, open our hearts more, and chip away at the unreasonable expectations we put on ourselves. We aren't perfect, but we are blessed to live this life, and we are better off being whole and real than fragmented and partially hidden. People will still accept and even love us exactly as we are, and those who don't didn't love the real us, and that's more than okay. When you understand how and choose to be the real you, you will have this powerful force called integrity by your side, every step you take, and that's a beautiful thing.

As I write these words to you, I can tell you I feel better about myself than I have in years. I feel confident, calm, and peaceful. I finally feel I am enough. Do I have my moments and days? Is there more I want to be, do, and have? Absolutely. But my quest is no longer coming from a place of needing more to satisfy a void. It's about owning my power and with a sense of curiosity and excitement, seeing what can come *out* of me, not *to* me.

In the months following the text conversation with my friend, I came to understand a few things that had a massive impact on my confidence, happiness, and sense of power:

-Our challenges can be external or internal. This book will help you master the internal challenges to equip you to deal with or alter the external to a more desirable set of circumstances. This involves stressing and worrying less, being less affected by and reactive to negativity, letting go of anger and regret, gaining clarity on what you truly desire, and understanding how to take empowered action to get what you want.

-Knowledge alone, without the right operating system, is useless. I held within me over a decade of intensive study of self-help, human behavior, and happiness and still felt like a failure. In the pages ahead, I offer you both the powerful knowledge and also the tools to upgrade your internal operating system. The two combined have the capacity to bring you remarkable and profound changes in how you feel about yourself and your life.

-If you feel you don't measure up, deal with frequent and/or pervasive self-doubt, or even achieve a great deal on the outside, but it never seems to fill the void within, you'll finally understand why and what to do about it. For good. No joke. #dropthemic

-Trying to banish your inner critic, despite the onslaught of the popular advice to do so, is a waste of energy and is self-defeating. She's never going away because she's part of you. I'll show you how to stop viewing her as the enemy, how to befriend her, and how to get her working on your behalf. It's easier than you think because the fact of the matter is, and you'll have to trust me on this right now (I'll prove it later,) she actually wants you to succeed.

-You have the ability, and I will show you how, to not only transcend negative experiences past or present but to turn them into valuable assets to support your desires and fulfill your purpose. You will learn how to firmly plant yourself as your center of gravity. Imagine having such a solid sense of self the actions of others can never again make you lose your balance or knock you off your feet.

My goal with this book is to help you come together as the full and complete you. There's a great sense of freedom and happiness to be found when that happens. You are about to understand what it means to be powerful and beautiful in an entirely new way.

Here is my solemn vow to you. The real you is far more beautiful, brilliant, and bursting with unrealized potential than any partial or masked version could ever be. When you finally get that, you will feel as if you've been away for a really long time, and you're finally home, safe, loved, and comfortable again in your own skin. Can you honestly think of anywhere you'd rather be?

I

Real is the New Black

We can't hate ourselves into a version of ourselves we can love.

-Lori Deschene

The question I asked my trusted friend that day as I lay
on my bed sobbing on a warm sunny day summed up my
internal battle. I knew I had a boatload of knowledge on
human behavior, law of attraction, happiness, and positive
psychology. What I could not understand was how I could
know so much, have life circumstances that many could only
wish for, yet feel so inadequate. *I was failing at being me.* How
do you even do that?

I had developed a significant belief system around what

it took to be happy. I believed what I learned to be true and accurate about what was required to live a happy and fulfilling life, but I myself wasn't happy. Everything I read and learned made sense to me. The fact that it wasn't having a positive impact on my own happiness? Not so much.

I questioned everything. Was my belief system wrong? Was I wrong in what I shared with others about happiness? Was I leading others down the wrong path? Was what I had learned inaccurate? Was everything I believed to be true, *not* true? What was I missing?

Drowning in a sea of confusion and about to go under, I prayed for a lifeline. I didn't need someone to rescue me. I'd pull myself out if I knew what I needed to do. *Just give me something, anything to grab onto that helps me understand. Because this shit? I'm done with it.*

By the grace of God, the Universe, Mother Nature, Source Energy, whatever this higher intelligence is, or maybe simply a well-targeted and timed Facebook ad, I came across a guy named Artie Wu. Artie is a brilliant, kind, and funny guy who also curses (a plus in my book.) He sold a couple of tech companies and then decided to follow his passion for teaching meditation and founded Preside Meditation[1]. Whatever he's offering, go get. Whatever he's selling that you can afford, buy. As of this writing, he doesn't have an affiliate program, so I ain't getting squat for sending you to him other than the satisfaction of knowing you will be better off as a result.

Through Artie's teachings, I finally understood the source of my internal conflict. Here's the analogy that he uses, and it is brilliant. Think of the complete you as a corporation governed by a board of directors. Each board member is a different aspect of you, all of which, when combined, make the unique and complete person you are. Each member or aspect of you is entitled to a seat at the table. They all belong. They all are needed. If you keep ignoring one of these board members or denying one or more a voice and place in your life, that member is going to get pissed.

Why would we ignore certain aspects of ourselves? Well, because doing so is a coping mechanism we learn as children because of inadvertent emotional wounds we suffer. If a well-meaning parent, teacher, or relative says something to us that we feel shames an aspect of ourselves, we then cut that part of us off and shoo it away as if it were an annoying pest. These comments or actions that cause us to do this could have something to do with our physical body or looks, our skills or competence, or even our identity. The example Artie often uses is say you are inherently creative and musical and want to be a musician but are repeatedly told you need to be a doctor or lawyer; you then believe you need to shut down and cut off your creative self. Being the great little kid you are and wanting to make your parents or caregivers proud, you send that aspect of yourself into exile.

Side note here, this is absolutely NOT about blaming whoever caused you to cut off a part of you. I firmly believe each of us does the best we can with what we have and know in any given moment. Besides, you have no idea what beliefs your parents were given when they were children.

What happens is we then unknowingly form lasting beliefs around these incidents that go on to affect us later in life. They become a sort of behind-the-scenes operating system that many of us are unaware even exist. Mine stared me in the face, but I couldn't see it. Have you ever had that happen? Had something, be it an understanding of a situation or even a container of creamer eye level in the fridge right smack in front of you, but you can't see it? (I've already come clean on that one.) In retrospect, it's so obvious that it's almost comical.

What do you suppose mine was? Based on what you've learned about me so far, what aspect of myself was I not allowing a role for in my life? What part of me did I deem unacceptable and ignored for so long that it was now emotionally bankrupting me? This is going to blow your mind. Sadness. Sounds crazy, right?

I believed sadness was a threat and would weaken me, so I resisted it at all costs. When I had a sad or negative thought, I'd get angry with it, wish it didn't exist, and shove it down. So not only did I have these sad thoughts, but I resented them and judged myself negatively for having them. *I'm Keryl, the positive person. These thoughts don't belong in my life.* As they say, what we resist, persists. The more I denied sadness and subsequently judged myself negatively for feeling it, the stronger the resistance I experienced between who I thought I *should* be on the outside, my mask, and what I really felt inside. It was like an emotional pressure cooker. Except I didn't explode. I imploded. I became small, weak, frightened, and withdrawn. I felt, for the second time in my life (as I wrote about in *Happy Bitch*) like a shell of myself. This time, because of what was going on inside me, not because of what was going on around me.

My denial of a genuine, human emotion was a denial of a legitimate part of me. I rendered myself incomplete, which is why none of the external circumstances were capable of making me feel like enough. This is what happens when we adorn ourselves with masks we believe we need to wear to be accepted, loved, and heard. Over time, we create a rift so big between our true selves and the ones we present to the outside world that we forget who we really are. Nothing we do is ever enough. We feel as if we don't even belong in our own lives. Maybe you can relate.

Some of these comments made to us or the actions of others close to us could be obvious and significant. Some may come to your mind right now. Others, as in my case, could be innocent, well-intended comments. When I was a kid, my mom always showed me love. She still does today. Even when I misbehaved as a child, she criticized the behavior but never withheld love from me. I consider myself very lucky to have her as my mom.

When I was upset and crying as a child and went to my mother like the whiney kid I was in that moment, she wouldn't listen to me until I sobered up. I'd be sobbing, blowing snot bubbles out of both nostrils, trying to explain why I was upset. How did she respond? "Turn it off!" she'd tell me firmly. She wouldn't engage in a conversation with me about why I was upset until I calmed down. Perfectly reasonable response, don't you think? I guarantee it was a better response than I would have had if I were in her shoes. How she handled it makes perfect sense. She didn't punish me or criticize me. She was trying to teach me something every child needs to learn—that crying and whining aren't how you get the results you want. Plus, how could she help me if she couldn't even understand me? That was her goal. She wanted to help me, and I completely misinterpreted our interaction.

So unbeknownst to me and certainly to my mother, I came to the conclusion that it's not okay to be sad and upset, and if you are, you will not be heard. *Excuse me, Sadness? Got a minute? You're fired.*

Here's the irony: The more I feared and denied sadness because I believed it was a threat, the more it weakened me and the more power it held *over* me, not in support of me. My futile efforts were like trying to deny my right arm as if it didn't belong to me, but my arm kept punching me in the face saying "I'm part of you, asshole! Quit denying me."

How crazy to imagine that allowing a place for sadness at the table would actually help me feel better! I know it sounds unbelievable, but if you dig a little deeper and put this in the right context, it makes sense. The brilliance that created us gave us everything we need. We aren't supposed to be something other than exactly what and who we are. To think otherwise is the grandest lie of all we tell ourselves. We come along, thinking we're the smart ones and can create a better version of ourselves by chipping away at the one God or the Universe created. What dipshits.

So I adopted and grew up with the identity of a positive person. You may ask, "Well, what's wrong with that? That's a good thing, isn't it?" Mostly, yes. Developing the mindset to overwhelmingly look for the positive does serve us very well. The problem only comes into play if it is taken to an extreme, which yours truly did in grand style. Remember, I created an entire belief system, identity, and career in which sadness could play no part.

How could I ever feel as if I were enough when I was denying a legitimate human emotion, a valid part of who I am?

Come to find out, I'm not alone. To varying degrees, we all do this.

What I also came to learn is that whatever part or parts of you that you may have mistakenly cut off don't want to dominate your life. They don't want to hurt or hold you back. They just want a voice. They want to be included. They want to *help you* show up in this world as the full and complete version of you. Is that not the position of power we all want? To show up each and every day, to ourselves and others as the most authentic version of ourselves? My God! What could be more liberating and empowering?

It turns out that everything I believed to be true about happiness *was* correct. It was just incomplete. *I* was incomplete. No amount of positive psychology, gratitude practice, or visualization could fix that. It could do wonders to the full operating version of us, but not the incomplete one.

Just like your right arm, all aspects of you are real and valid. Not only real and valid, but you *need* them to feel whole, right in your life and function to your highest abilities.

So now your question is, *How do I find out if I've cut off a part of me, and then how do I reconcile with that part?*

All you need is a little patience and trust in your inner wisdom. What I am about to share is an abbreviated version of the process Artie took me through and my own account of it. It will absolutely get you started. For a more in-depth experience, visit www.presidemeditation.com.

Keep in mind, this is a compassionate exercise. Don't force it or fear it. It's about you coming into your own. Consider it simply having a conversation. You can do that, can't you? Think of it as more of a curious exercise and allow it to unfold, much like a flower that opens up and blooms, showing the world its beauty.

Find a place where you can sit quietly and uninterrupted for a few minutes. Take a couple of deep breaths and ask yourself, "Who is my missing board member? What part of me did I reject or do I feel ashamed of?" Another clue for you if you aren't getting an answer right away is to ask "Where in my life am I struggling?"

Here's the big one: "Where in my life did I come to believe "I'll only be lovable if _____?""

Then relax and wait for it. I promise you the answer is within you. Don't be afraid of it. It may sting a little, but the relief you will ultimately feel and power you will gain will far outweigh anything that comes up. You can do this with your eyes closed or the way I do it, by writing out the question and then the answer. I assure you this process can be very liberating. It may be scary and painful, but you will feel lighter and one big step closer to feeling like you again once you do. It's like ripping a Band-Aid off and allowing some fresh air to help heal your wound.

You may recall a specific incident from your childhood, or you may just get a strong sense of something that makes you say "Holy shit! That makes so much sense!" Don't let your brain get over-involved here and second guess what comes up. Trust your first answer(s).

When you get an answer, check in with how it feels. It's not just about what makes sense. It's also about what answer feels right. You may get one or you may get many. I wouldn't try to reinstate the whole board room at once, so if you get more than one, trust your intuition and choose one to focus on and work with first.

Once you've identified a part of you that you cut off because you felt you needed to in order to be loved or a successful you, then ask "If I reinstated this board member and allowed it to influence my life, how would I be different in this world? What would change?" Then see if you're okay with that answer. It may not mean you suddenly make a major shift in direction. It could be a matter of beginning to incorporate new practices or even simply seeing yourself, your choices, and life through a new lens and see what comes from that.

If you are comfortable and choose to, you can do what I did, which was to take it a step further and actually engage in dialogue with this part of yourself. Again, I found writing out the questions and answers worked best. You can even name or give initials to that part of you as well. So for example, let's call my missing board member SK for Sad Keryl. Here are the questions I asked:

- Hello, SK, are you okay?
- Are you hurt? How?
- Are you angry?
- Do you have a message for me?
- What do you fear most deeply?
- Do you ever feel that I love you conditionally, only if you _____? When do you feel this? How do I do this to

[handwritten margin note, top:] I think once we tap in more with our heavenly father, then we will feel all those things.

[handwritten header:] Keryl Pesce

you?

- What do you need me to do differently going forward?
Keep in mind, this part of you doesn't want or need to
dictate and control everything. You are the Chairwoman of
the Board. So depending on the answers you get, you can
engage in a sort of negotiation. Find out what that member
needs and make agreements with it that serve you both. I
know it sounds crazy, but I need you to trust me on this.

It is a powerful exercise. I *immediately* felt better, more
complete, relaxed, and confident. Ultimately, I discovered I
should not fear feeling sad, and allowing space for it would
allow me to show up more authentically, more confident, and
better equipped to do what I came here to do.

[handwritten margin note:] This result is temp. w/out God.

Just as I now look back on the pain and struggle from
my divorce with gratitude for how it helped me grow, shape
my life and share the experiences and lessons learned with
others, I view my experience of exiling sadness the same. I
am better as a result. I can help you as a result. In hindsight, it
was a gift I unwrapped and now get to share with you.

Something else you will love about this: The part of you
that you cut off is also a *major* source of the negative voice
you have in your head. That's the one who tries to tell you
that you aren't good enough, makes you afraid to make a
decision, try something, or criticizes you when you do make a
mistake. What I want you to understand is we ALL have it.
Even the Dalai Lama deals with it. But the powerful understanding I came to through this process was this voice, as
annoying and mean as it can be, actually *wants* you to succeed.
It's afraid you won't be successful, so it's trying to correct
what it sees as wrong with you or your actions. It just doesn't

22

always go about it in the most productive way. Basically, it has good intentions but can be an asshole about it.

Just this understanding *alone* changes the game. We think there is something wrong with us for having the voice of negativity and try to crush it or eliminate it. Good luck with that. It's not going to happen. Instead, once you understand it really is there to help you, you can listen to it and actually engage with it, rather than trying to shut it up.

So when the voice of doubt and negativity comes up, pause and have a conversation with it. "What is your message for me? What is it you want *for* me?" Then listen for the answer. You will ultimately discover it wants you to succeed. You can then come to an agreement with it. For example, you can acknowledge its intention is to help but gain agreement that it will speak to you with respect and constructively rather than critically. Then when that bitchy voice creeps back in, you can say, "Okay, hold on a minute. We agreed to handle this differently." Don't be afraid to stop and write these conversations out. They are great to refer back to and doing so helps you clear your head. Get it out of your head and on paper and make room for clarity.

Also keep in mind, this part of you may have been shunned and exiled for a long time. It might be a bit shy and afraid to come to the surface, so be patient. If you don't get an answer right away, don't sweat it and don't force it. Let it go. Do something you enjoy and try again later.

In addition to feeling more grounded, complete, and confident, I began to approach my life a little differently. No longer afraid of sadness (ironically, my fear actually gave more power to it,) if I watch a sad scene in a movie, I allow myself

Kenya Pesce

to cry. It is a release. It feels good. With family and friends, I am no longer as quick to immediately turn the conversation positive if they feel down. I allow space to hear them, meet them where they are in that feeling, and if appropriate, more softly move the conversation toward the bright side or a solution. I feel closer to them, as if I am showing up in a more loving way. I feel better equipped to show up here for you in this book as well.

Here is the ridiculously cool thing about this process. Not only will you feel better, happier, more authentic, and confident, in other words, not only will you go from feeling incomplete to more complete, you will unleash *incredible* reserves of power. You have been using a *shit load* of energy denying this part of you, and now you will free up that energy to take yourself and your life where you truly want to go.

In addition, this part of you is now operating on your behalf to support you in your desires and goals. It will help you see more clearly the direction of your life, and make better, wiser decisions. With your board member(s) reinstated, you've now got a complete and fully equipped team to guide you and support you. All of you having your own back. Pretty awesome, don't you think?

Bringing the whole you together, having the courage and wisdom to present the full and complete you to yourself and the world, is simultaneously liberating and empowering beyond imagination.

There's nothing wrong with any part of you. Your wholeness is your rightness. Your wholeness is your beautifulness. There is so much within you waiting to come alive, greet, and have an impact on the world, in a way that no one else could. It's as if the real you is a Phoenix rising from the ashes—bright, brilliant, and powerful. That's about as beautiful as it gets.

Beauty Regimen

Carve out some private time to welcome aspects of yourself back into your life.

Keryl Pesce

2

It's Okay to Not Be Okay

It took me a long, long time to realize we are not meant to be perfect. We're meant to be whole.

-Jane Fonda

In case you haven't noticed, we live in a time when thinking positive is the attitude de jour. Much like a Michael Kors handbag, skinny jeans with folded hems or sling-back pumps, we adorn ourselves with the latest style of attitude we must wear to look good and be accepted. Make no mistake. Positive thinking is in. Good vibes only. Dream big. Choose happiness. Feeling low about yourself or your circumstances? So yesterday. You might as well tease your hair four inches high, put on blue eye shadow, and wear shoulder pads. This is the latest version of "You can't sit at our table at lunch unless you bring good vibes," inadvertently resulting in a form of emotional shaming where it's not okay to not be okay. As a result, our pain gets shoved down and hidden, giving it everything it needs to fester and grow.

I realize I sound like a drag but hang with me for a second. I am absolutely an advocate of looking for the good in situations, others and ourselves. I believe wholeheartedly in the incredible power each of us has to choose our perspective and responses in any given situation. There are immense benefits to our emotional and physical state, to others around us, as well as the circumstances surrounding us by choosing to look for the good. But here's the catch. If it is forced positivity and in conflict with how you truly feel inside, you're offering up a load of bullshit to yourself and the universe and not only will it *not* help you, there's a good chance you'll dig yourself deeper into a pit of ick, a swampy, heavy mess of low self-worth, self-doubt, fear, and sadness. Why? *Because you're living a lie.* And you bring that lie with you everywhere. You know it and whether the people around you consciously realize it or not, they do too.

Constantly forcing our thoughts to the positive when in reality we feel like crap creates internal conflict. We begin to feel like frauds. And in a way, we are. We put a smile on our face while crying inside.

Do I believe we can benefit from guiding our thoughts towards positive outcomes? You bet. No question. But here's the catch. Don't deny, or worse, *judge*, the reality of what you feel in the moment first. Otherwise, you compound the problem. Trust me on this. I was a first-rate disaster doing exactly this.

Here's how that goes down. First, we have a negative emotion, which doesn't feel great to begin with. Then we add to the situation with the judgment of "I shouldn't feel negative emotions, so what's wrong with me that I do? I focus on the positive. Why isn't it helping? WTF is wrong with me?" Then we feel like a double failure because we feel like shit, and then we feel like shit about feeling like shit? Follow? We're basically, with good intentions, creating our very own personal shit show. And nobody wants that ticket.

Yes, I am an advocate of looking for the good in situations, others and ourselves. I also believe we wouldn't be given the ability to experience sadness, anger, fear or any of their other "negative" counterparts if they didn't somehow serve us. We've taken a potentially helpful approach of positive thinking to an extreme, and by not allowing ourselves the healthy experiencing and expression of all emotions and beating ourselves up for feeling them, we unknowingly amplify the very experiences we want to avoid.

Look for the good in situations, but don't do so rigidly and as a cover up to what you truly feel or you've got a recipe for prolonged struggle, internal and external conflict, and possible breakdown. This I know first hand. I worked myself up (or should I say down) into one major hot mess doing so.

As I discussed in the last chapter, I spent many years viewing sadness as my arch nemesis, fighting it whenever it showed up, shoving it down and fearful of it playing any role in my life. And what happened? The harder I worked at pushing it away, the worse it affected me. In the last chapter, the context of sadness in my life was about the bigger picture of any aspect of ourselves we deem unacceptable and "fire" from a role in our lives. As I said, it could be an emotional aspect, a gender aspect, a natural inclination toward creativity–just about anything. But in this chapter, I want to dig deeper into the idea of the reality of negative experiences, more particularly, negative emotions such as sadness, anger and fear and how we can view and respond to them in a way that better serves us.

Can we begin by agreeing that Mother Nature ain't no dummy? I mean think about it. You plant a tomato seed in dirt, fertilize and water it regularly, and a few months later, you've got a plant as tall as you that bears delicious, mouth-watering tomatoes. If you took the time element out of it, it's really kind of magical. Nothing around it became less as a result. The soil didn't diminish. None of us had any less sunshine as a result. A fruitful plant grew seemingly from nothing. It's remarkable. And don't get me started on the fact that this flat thing we call the ground that we walk on is actually the surface of a huge sphere that rotates every 24 hours and is hurtling through space around the sun at 600-plus miles an hour. The result of which, we get night and day, seasons and gravity. If she didn't know what she was doing, we'd freeze up or fry up or fall off planet earth. I can't deny she can be a pain in the ass sometimes, particularly when it comes to (ahem) aging, but her intelligence is beyond comprehension to us humans. From the highest view possible, we can begin to consider how brilliant Mother Nature (God, Universe–I use these terms interchangeably) is, and realize its design *supports* life and growth. for HIM!

So if we've been equipped with not only the ability to feel excitement, joy, and love, but also the ability to experience sadness, anger, and fear, maybe there's a reason. Maybe these "negative" emotions aren't the enemy. Maybe they serve a purpose. And maybe, just maybe, we defy the laws of nature when we try to deny the reality of those feelings, ultimately exacerbating the feelings we wanted to avoid in the first place. You can pause here and process for a moment if need be. It's a biggie.

Each time you push down a negative feeling like anger or sadness, you haven't made it go away. All you've done is made it go deeper inside. You might temporarily quiet it and get a bit of relief, but it's still there. And the next time you push down a negative emotion you deem unacceptable, it finds the last one you shoved down and joins forces with it, like a quiet little army gaining in power, waiting to attack. It keeps building and getting stronger. Then one day the clerk at the drive-through hands you a cup of tea with two tea bags in it when you specifically asked for one, and you lose your shit. Maybe you scream at her, or maybe you scream out loud as you drive away, convinced all people are stupid, your entire day will now suck, nothing goes right for you . . . ever . . . FML.

If you've ever wondered why the little things set you off, this is why. It isn't about the little things. It's about the many valid feelings you shoved down and denied . . . and judged. Maybe you don't have anger issues. Maybe you aren't chronically depressed. Maybe you've simply assumed all negative emotions are bad, therefore shouldn't exist, and never allowed yourself to experience and express them in a healthy way. Do you really think we would be equipped with anger, sadness, and fear if they didn't somehow serve us? I'm not saying focus on them and float around in them like a pool noodle that's found its forever home in an algae-filled abandoned pool. I swam in that mess. It ain't pretty. I'm saying quit being so afraid, judgmental and in denial of genuine human emotions.

So many of us are surrounding ourselves with positive sayings and affirmations on the outside, feeling like crap on the inside. People tell you to stand in front of the mirror and keep repeating how amazing you are, and you'll finally feel like it. Maybe that works for some people. It never has for me. If I feel like a loser and look at myself saying "I'm awesome," I feel like a liar. Now I feel like a loser AND a liar. I end up feeling worse.

We have come to believe we are tough and strong by covering up and ignoring our wounds. *Denial is not helping you.* At all. You're better off acknowledging how you feel, allowing space for it and letting it flow through you. You're better off letting it out than pushing it down. Cause that shit will come up at some point. And if you don't manage it in a healthy, productive way, it can wreak some major havoc in your life, wallet, body, and relationships. Maybe it already has. But it's okay because here you are learning something very powerful about yourself. Here you are, finally understanding why you've struggled. Here you are, perhaps not a moment too soon, taking some much-needed pressure off of yourself.

Inhale. Now exhale. Let's continue.

There is nothing more empowering and confidence boosting than feeling capable of solving our problems and moving our lives in a better direction. This is a skill we cannot develop until we first allow the space for the negative feelings and then make productive use of them. They carry information. They carry messages. And we'll never hear what they have to tell us if we judge them all as worthless and detrimental and deny our right to experience them. Negative emotions are valid. Period. They are feedback that something in your life needs addressing. You face a challenge that you need to figure out or overcome. When you see them for what they really are, you stop fighting against them and begin to *use* them. The beautiful thing is as you do, you learn to take intelligent, productive action toward something better, minus the resistance. And guess what happens each time you do that? Your happiness, sense of peace, faith, and confidence grow . . . sometimes by leaps and bounds.

Fighting against your emotions and beating yourself up for feeling them takes a crapload of energy. As you learn to allow, learn from, and trust your emotions, you free up incredible amounts of energy you can now put toward increasing your physical and emotional strength and your ability to achieve your dreams. This one change in your understanding and how you approach and deal with your emotions could have a massive impact on the quality of your life . . . immediately, as in this minute. It's you, stepping into your alternate universe.

Your first step is to acknowledge there is nothing wrong with you if you experience negative emotions. I'm not saying become a martyr and hang out on Negativity Avenue. You don't want to stay there. What you want to do is not fight it. What you want to do is not judge yourself as failing at life because there are days when you cry or want to throat punch people. Give yourself permission to feel what you genuinely feel, absent of judgment.

You will discover something pretty interesting when you do so. When you stop giving so much power to avoiding the negative emotions, their intensity and duration lessen. As I previously mentioned, what we resist persists.

You can get from feeling like crap and incomplete to feeling like enough and confident. No question. But it's a process, not a transaction. We've made it transactional. "Have a negative thought and feeling? Replace it! Boom! Happy life." Not really. It's more about flow, an allowance.

My father passed away a few years ago, and my mother had been living alone in my childhood home which is about twenty minutes from me. She recently sold her home and moved 12 hours away. It was a good move and the right one for her. It sucked for me. I had to let go of having her near me, which was the case my entire life. It was hard to say goodbye to my mother. I know she's still alive, and I can call her on the phone and talk with her. I am grateful for all that. It still ripped my heart out.

Not only was I dealing with her moving, but I was dealing with letting go of my childhood home and all of the memories and emotional attachments I had to it. After she left, I walked through her empty house, room by room, recalling many of my childhood memories. All of the Christmas mornings, coming down the hall and seeing our Christmas tree with presents for my sisters and me, lying in bed in the room I shared with one of my sisters as my grandmother stood in the doorway softly singing us lullabies in

German when she babysat for us, sleepovers with friends in junior high, eating popcorn, drinking Kool-Aid and watching Saturday Night Live. I went there. It felt like a 50-pound weight on my chest. I sat at the kitchen table and cried my eyes out. I went where it hurt with courage. I gave myself permission to feel it all. It wasn't fun, and it certainly didn't feel great, but it offered me a healthy release. Understand this: what we don't process gets stored.

Don't deny your negative feelings. Alchemize them. You have this incredible power to transform the crap in your life into gold . . . in a very literal sense.

Once you give yourself permission, allow space in your life to feel these emotions, you fear them less and they benefit you more. Empower yourself to receive the benefit. How? By becoming curious. By trusting they have shown up to teach you something, that they carry with them messages and lessons that will serve you well. Ask what message your negative emotions have for you. Actually dialogue with them. Do it in your head or write it out.

Here are two powerful questions to ask: "How can I grow and expand in the face of this? What positive action can I take?" Then move toward positive thinking and action. Positive thinking is fabulous. Positive action is even better. Ask yourself what step, what action can you take today, right now, to move yourself closer to how you want to feel and what you want to experience.

It's important for you to understand closer is good, *really* good. Because sometimes we feel so desperately low, that happiness and self-confidence seem light years away. They feel so completely out of reach, we can't fathom ever getting there. Sometimes reaching for a little better is *exactly* what you need, because anyone can reach for a little better. Don't put the weight of the world on your shoulders to get out of your funk with a snap of your fingers and all of a sudden, you feel great. No one becomes obese over one big meal. Nor does anyone lose 40 or 50 pounds overnight. It's a process. Sometimes feeling better is too, and that's more than okay.

Feeling happy and confident is not about a living a trouble-free life where you feel only positive emotions 24/7. Setting up that expectation is unrealistic. Happiness is about being confident in your ability to creatively solve your challenges and achieve your goals. You only get there by doing something about what upsets you in a productive way. You can't do that if you deny yourself the right to feel valid emotions to begin with and then look for the nuggets of wisdom they hold.

By the way, all anger stems from pain or fear of experiencing more of it. So even the anger you feel is justified, although call forth wisdom in how you express it. Don't be an asshole about it. Causing more pain for yourself or someone else isn't going to heal your pain. That's picking at the scab.

Each time you transform a negative emotion into positive action, you reinforce your self-confidence. That's a loop you want to get in on. It's a major power play.

There's something else I want you to consider here. Knowing what you now do, how will it change how you interact with others around you when they are angry or sad? Think about it. How will you now show up for people you care about when they are upset? I used to be the one who would immediately try to shift the thinking of the people around me if they were talking or feeling negative. I realize now how it could be annoying, potentially detrimental, and actually create a rift between them and me.

A friend of mine recently posted something on social media to the effect of "When I'm drowning, words of encouragement won't help me." I used to think instant positivity was the answer, not only for myself but whenever someone I cared about was upset. Now I understand this instant application of positive carries with it an underlying message, one that can amplify our negative feelings. "There's something wrong with you for feeling this way. You are failing right now because you shouldn't feel the way you do. You are not justified in your feelings." Honestly, how helpful is that? It's not.

interesting

I had a bad day a while back. And by "bad day," I mean name a negative thought or emotion, and it had its grip on me. It felt like a full-body invasion. I could barely hold back the tears. I don't remember what started it or what the negative thoughts even were. I just remember how awful I felt, what a complete loser of a human being I felt like. My husband, God love him, is wonderful, kind and supportive. He sensed where I was, asked why I was feeling so down and as I tried to explain, he responded with the logical reasons why I shouldn't feel what I was feeling. I then defended my position and why I had the right to feel so shitty. He grew frustrated and flat out told me I shouldn't think like that. I get it. From a logical standpoint, he was correct. But at that moment, I was barely hanging on. What I did not need was what I perceived as the invalidation of my feelings. It was the classic feeling like crap, then feeling like crap about feeling like crap I mentioned earlier. He intended to help. I know his intentions were in the right place. I ended up locked in the bathroom sobbing on the floor.

It's not only important to give yourself permission to be sad or afraid or pissed off, give that permission to others as well. I am not suggesting you encourage negative thinking and allow people you care about to wallow in self-pity. I am suggesting you allow them space for it, just as you will for yourself. Meet them where they are, then more softly guide them out of it by asking questions. Don't tell them how to feel or what to think. Try something like this "I understand why you feel like you do. I probably would too. And I know what you feel right now doesn't feel so great. So what can we do to move you in a better direction? What do you prefer to this, and what action can we take toward that?" Or maybe simply "I understand how you feel," without trying to fix it at all. You will serve them infinitely better than if you force positivity on them. Remember, it's a process, not a transaction.

I strongly believe we're better off not putting on a happiness mask all the time and acknowledge that being human is sometimes messy and unfair. And when we feel the messy parts of life, we stop the bullshit of thinking there is something wrong with us that makes us uniquely qualified for misfortune and start allowing space for being human. What if we stop fighting against what we feel isn't fair or not good enough about us or our lives and instead, allow those things to shape us? To position us to do and experience what we came here for. Wherever you are, however far you feel you

[left margin handwritten note: This will help me be more compassionate]

are from what you want, even if that simply is to feel at home in your own skin again, you are never too far away. Ever. Or you wouldn't still be here. Begin wherever you are with whatever you've got. I've got your back.

You are neither flawed nor weak because you feel sad, afraid or angry. The only flaw here is in believing you are. And in that belief, you keep your wounds hidden under the Band-Aid of denial with a smile on your face you don't feel in your heart. I don't believe in faking it 'til you make it. Putting on a fake smile or positive front you don't genuinely feel doesn't heal you at the source. It doesn't allow you to pull out the emotional splinter *that is not you*. It's not part of you. It doesn't belong to you. What belongs to you is the responsibility to remove the splinter or get help doing it if you need it. What belongs to you is the responsibility to get in there and dig it out despite your fear, and begin the process of becoming a stronger, more resilient version of yourself. What belongs to you is your story. That includes the truth of the past, of who you are and what you have yet to write.

More important, what belongs to you is the meaning you choose to attach to that story. Will it become "I am flawed. I am being punished. I am a victim."? Or can you acknowledge your hurt without shame or blame, pull out of you what hurt you but isn't you, and figure out how to contribute to your life, the lives of those you love or will love or have never met?

The meaning is an act of creation on your part. And for every minute, sleepless night, year or decade you've spent wondering your purpose here on earth. This is it . . . the meaning you attach and the subsequent action you take as a result of your pain.

Sometimes holding back your tears, holds you back. Sometimes being okay with not being okay simultaneously liberates you and puts you on a direct path to discovering both your humanness, your wholeness, and your purpose.

Be brave. Explore the dark caverns of what you've spent enormous amounts of time and energy wishing away or hating. Your pain is not something to escape. It's your portal. It's guiding you toward the light you seek.

Beauty Regimen

Find someplace private and where you feel safe.
In a notepad or journal, write a
letter to "Life" and vent your anger or hurt.
Don't hold back. Don't feel guilty. Be truthful.
Then close your eyes and imagine the
most loving part of you separates from you and
comes to comfort you, making you feel
loved and supported. You may experience this
as a feeling, or if she has something to say,
write it down.

3

Emerge and See

Within you is destiny waiting to be born.

-Derek Rydall

Do you often feel as if the crap that has happened to you has put you at a disadvantage in life? Do you look around at others you feel are baggage free and wonder if you'll ever have the capacity to live the life you desire . . . as if you and your life are somehow flawed? If you answered "Yes," this chapter is for you.

As I discovered, certain practices truly do help cultivate a happy life. Focusing our attention on what's right with us and the world, choosing what we feed our minds, whom we surround ourselves with, to name a few, are all elements that contribute to our happiness.

However certain foundational requirements must first be met or these practices will not give us the kind of results we desire. As I shared, denying and fighting against a valid aspect of myself essentially rendered all other knowledge and practices useless. So does the denial of genuine human emotions. There's another equally powerful pre-requisite that has a massive impact on your happiness, confidence, and enjoyment of life, and that is your perspective on and responses you choose to the challenges you face.

How can you successfully practice the Law of Attraction to make boatloads of money, marry a rock star or own a five-bedroom home on the ocean if you are loaded with the baggage associated with hanging on to anger and regret? It's just not going to happen. What does happen is that you feel even *more* like a failure because these practices work for everyone else and not you. Any of this sounding at all familiar?

Crafting a vision for your future, being grateful, focusing on what you want and being kind to others are all powerful practices. If, and it's a BIG FAT IF, you have first dealt with the stuff that gets in the way. You need a solid foundation first.

You've heard of Maslow's hierarchy of needs, right? How can we think about self-actualization if we haven't yet met our basic survival needs of having enough to eat? Similarly, how can we truly benefit from daily practices designed to enhance our enjoyment of life if we're all wadded up with anger and regret and barely surviving emotionally? It's like walking up to a starving person and suggesting they create a dream board with images of food. Are you kidding me?

I made a solemn vow to you in the introduction that the real and whole version of you is by far the most powerful one and the most beautiful one. I'll make another: If you haven't already, you will deal with crap you won't ask for or deserve. Guaranteed. It's going to happen. Ah, the whole me is such a buzz kill, isn't she?

Look, you just can't avoid the fact that shit is gonna go down. It will. But the anger and regret associated with it is something *you* choose to attach to it. There is what happens to you, and then there is who you are in relationship to it. There are unfair and unfortunate circumstances and actions of others, and then there is your choice in how they affect you and what you do with them. Your life is not the luck of the draw. You may have been dealt what you feel is a crappy hand, but play it smart and you can still win. If you bitch, complain and blame and hold a death grip on your right to be angry and hurt, you will lose every time. Choosing to stay angry and resentful is totally and completely stacking the cards against yourself.

I realize this may seem a bit contradictory to Chapter 2. There is a massive difference between allowing space to feel genuine emotions without judging them and living in the place 24/7. Allow, experience, release. If you're having trouble with the releasing part, this chapter ought to help.

I get that you've been hurt and have every right to feel the way you do. I've been there. I understand. I also know that there is a part of you that feels safer in your anger as if it somehow protects you from being hurt or taken advantage of again. But that's not how it works. One of my favorite quotes of all time is by Nelson Mandela. He said, "Resentment is like drinking poison and hoping it will kill your enemy." Your prolonged anger doesn't keep you safe. As a matter of fact, it's doing the exact opposite. You think it's protecting you from outside threats, but in reality, it's killing you from the inside out. How about we do something about that?

Come with me for a little trip back in time. Let's go all the way back to before you were even born. In fact, let's go to the precise instant you were first conceived. At the exact moment, two microscopic organisms came together, *the entire code was written to build you.* All the information needed to grow the unique, miracle of a human being that you are, existed at conception. *Everything.* Every bit of information for you to develop from something too small for the naked eye to see into the never-before-alive, walking, talking, breathing, miracle of a human being you are, complete with all functioning organs and systems materialized. That's some impressive act of creation, wouldn't you agree?

Stop and think about that for a second. First you can't even see the thing with your naked eyes, and nine months later, a human being comes wailing its way into the world. I know women grow babies all the time, but come on! It's crazy when you think about it. Have you ever wondered how that is possible? Where does that information come from? Who or what has the capacity to make that happen? Call it God, Mother Nature, the Universe, whatever suits the beliefs you hold. Let's look at whatever it is in the context of a form of intelligence.

Regardless of what God you pray to or none at all, the

truth of the matter is *there is an intelligence at work beyond our comprehension.* What does this have to do with the challenges I promised you'll endure?

Here are two significant facts true of all life on this planet, including yours:

1– Everything you need to actualize your full potential already exists within you. The code was written the second you were conceived.

2- This intelligence designs all things *for*, not *against* life and growth.

In his powerful book *Emergence*[2], Derek Rydall makes a convincing case for the above using an oak tree as an example. Let's explore this for a minute, because the fact of the matter is the same brilliance that wrote your code, wrote the code for a bulldog, a goldfish, and a parsnip.

How does the life of an oak tree begin? Not by picking one up at your local nursery, grabbing a shovel, digging a hole, and tossing in a little dried cow poop. It starts out as a tiny green acorn. The very first thing that needs to happen for that acorn to actualize its full potential and become the grand oak tree it is destined to become is to get buried in dirt. It basically has to hang around for a bit, hidden from the outside world in the protective cover of darkness, kind of like you and I first had to do. Then what happens? It doesn't pop its little acorn head above ground reaching for the sky, growing limbs and eager to make babies of its own. If it tried to achieve such success as a tree too quickly without first establishing a root system, it'd be screwed, right? The first time the wind blows, the rain comes or the sun shines, it will topple over, get washed away, or shrivel up. The tree doesn't

God works all things together for the good of those who love him.

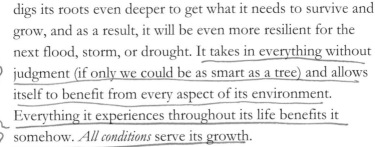

resent the wind, storms, and rain or even droughts. It simply digs its roots even deeper to get what it needs to survive and grow, and as a result, it will be even more resilient for the next flood, storm, or drought. It takes in everything without judgment (if only we could be as smart as a tree) and allows itself to benefit from every aspect of its environment. Everything it experiences throughout its life benefits it somehow. *All conditions* serve its growth.

You: So Keryl, you're telling me that all my potential exists within me already?

Me: Yes.

You: You're telling me that all my experiences, both those I perceive as positive and negative, ultimately serve my capacity to grow, live, and thrive?

Me: Yes.

You: Do you mean to tell me that my difficult past experiences don't put me at a disadvantage? They actually positively serve my infinite potential? My purpose in life?

Me: Bingo. Not only do they serve you, but the more you have struggled in the past, the deeper your roots have dug, and the more poised you are to achieve greatness. By the undeniable laws of nature, it cannot be any other way.

You: Holy shit! This changes everything.

Me: Sure does. Hello alternate universe.

All along (as I did for far too freaking long) you've wondered what you're doing wrong, whether or not you'll figure things out, find happiness, achieve your goals, and feel like enough. All along, you've resented your troubles, road-blocks, and all the "unfair" crap life has thrown your way. Dig in, baby. You have strong-ass roots and are only a few new insights away from a major, kick-ass growth spurt.

First, you need to understand and accept that everything that has and will come to you in the form of people or experiences has the capacity to serve you. *Everything.* But you gotta stop fighting the reality of the moment and *certainly* stop playing the regret tapes of the past. Those are like underground worms gnawing away at your roots. Ain't nobody got time for that. As you stay pissed off at others or the invisible conspiracy you believe exists to screw up your life and happiness, you stunt your growth. You may be alive, but you exist as a tiny fraction of the extraordinary you that is possible . . . the truly beautiful you . . . the one that is *already* in you waiting to emerge. Not until you dig in, realize everything you have experienced and will experience has the capacity to serve you, and accept the nutrient-rich benefits (read, crap that happens to you) into your being and life, will you reach your ultimate, within-you-already, capacity and purpose.

You must begin to let go of the idea that the shit that happened shouldn't have happened. It did. Guess what percent of the time you lose when you argue with reality? 100%.

It's time to stop wishing for the impossible so you can focus on the possible. Are you with me?

Everything you need to live out your fullest potential comes *from* you, not *to* you. Your deepest desires are not things you need to attract, achieve, or get, or for that matter, even worry if they'll ever materialize. Your deepest desires are a glimmer of what is already in you waiting for the right conditions to emerge. Your deepest desires are full and authentic self-expression.

You are perfectly made, brilliant, and loaded with infinite potential. Right now. This instant. To think anything less is doubting the force/intelligence/God that created you.

I'm not going to say life can't be a bitch sometimes. It can . . . a roaring, raging, hormonal, imbalanced, hangry bitch! But if you can wrap your beautiful mind around the fact that whatever you go through has the capacity to make you stronger and allow you to grow taller and more magnificent, you will view and respond to what happens to you in a very different way. As a result, you open up a world of possibilities. Think about it. No one who has ever achieved greatness, defined both by living a fulfilling life and making a positive impact, did so without first dealing with and growing from the significant challenges they faced.

If we think we are unlucky or being punished, what do we do? Complain, feel sorry for ourselves, and stay stuck, unhappy, and resentful. It keeps us small and stunts our growth. Yes, shit happens. I'll give you that. It happens to all of us. But what happens to you does not have to define you. *You are not what happens to you.* You are how you choose to respond. You are who you choose to become as a result.

When you open up to a new way of looking at the most difficult experiences of your life, you develop the capacity to respond differently. If you stop assuming life is a complete bitch (she does have her moments,) that illnesses, job losses, accidents, betrayals should never happen, and if they do, the only way to respond is to hate and resent them, you put the power over your life outside of your own hands. Everyone deals with crap they neither ask for nor deserve. Everyone. Those who truly become successful have simply learned to *leverage*, not resist the realities they face.

If we stop resisting the reality of what is at the moment, trust what we experience will somehow serve us and choose wise responses, our lives can become meaningful and powerful. As you do this more and more, you begin to notice situations and opportunities appear right before your eyes that are better than anything you could have imagined. It's like reaching your hand out, opening it wide, and your magic wand flies right in. You realize you are not a victim of life but the creator of your life. The power to choose your responses, baby. That's what I'm talking about.

It begins with the shift in the way you see the tough stuff that happens to you, understanding that the Universe/ God/Mother Nature has your back, has positioned you for life and growth, and everything that you experience serves that purpose.

Once you stop resisting and hating the reality of your experiences, the key is to then figure out how to leverage your conditions to your benefit. Wanna know how? Cool. Chin up, straighten your crown and let's keep going.

Take my FAQ approach.

F: Here's where my second-favorite "f" word comes in. You and me, if we want to expand our ability to become who we are destined to become and be, do, and have everything we desire to live extraordinary lives, *must* learn to FORGIVE. Don't roll your eyes. If you want to live a truly happy, productive, fulfilling, and joyful life, you honestly don't have a choice in the matter. It's a pre-requisite. Hanging on to anger and resentment is a major block to happiness and thief of your power. Not only does it seriously stunt your growth, weaken you physically, emotionally and intellectually, but it literally puts your life at risk.

A & Q: Then, you ASK new QUESTIONS.

So how do you do it? How do you release and let go of all that angst in you that you have every right to feel? You allow yourself to feel it fully and then wrap it, like the gift it can be, in compassion. It begins with what we already covered—the basic understanding that all conditions serve you, and what doesn't serve you is fighting reality or playing the same angry tapes of the past.

Get yourself somewhere where you are not at risk of someone hearing you and calling 911 for a "girl-gone-loony situation." Privacy, please.

Look, I know we don't want to dig up old wounds. I know they hurt, and our instinct is to not think about them, try to forget or ignore them, hoping over time they will lose their power over us. I get it. But what we don't heal doesn't go away. It festers, gets infected, and spreads.

Let's get in there and clean up the wound. It may sting, but the healing that comes from this is so worth it. Be brave, bite your lip if you need to, and let's continue.

Once you are somewhere private, close your eyes and pull up the memory that burns your ass, the one you wish never happened. It could be a situation or experience, the actions of another person or possibly even something you did that you are mad at yourself for. Pull that up in your mind. Put it front and center and vent as if your life depends on it. You can do that out loud, in writing or simply imagine yourself feeling that rage and expressing everything you need to. Let it all out.

Then take a few deep breaths and turn on the curiosity. How can I introduce some compassion here? If it's another person, imagine what he or she must have experienced in his or her lifetime, particularly childhood, that would influence his or her choices? What pain did he experience? Was she lacking love in her childhood? It actually helps to imagine the person as a child. Feel appreciation that you yourself aren't in a place where you'd do what this person did. And if it's you that you're mad at, throw your arms around yourself. Show yourself some love and compassion. The fact is we are mostly clueless as to the subconscious programs running our respective shows.

Then forgive into love and compassion. Keep shifting your perspective and asking different questions until you are able to do so. Now, if you suffered greatly, it may take a few tries to get there. Be patient. This is not about brute force. Remember, sometimes a little progress is all you need. Each time you do this successfully, you gain clarity and confidence. It is simultaneously a major release and a coming together. You will feel lighter and at the same time, more grounded.

After you've done this a time or two or twenty, you want to put your experiences inside the frame of faith that they will serve you somehow and ask future-based questions. You are choosing to let go of "Why me?" and instead choosing "What's next?" The questions we ask are *powerful* acts of creation. Ask yourself "What good can come from this? What good can I do with this? How can I live an even better existence because of this? How can I find a way that my response to this experience benefits others?"

If you read my first book, you know my ex's affair,

which devastated me at the time, became the impetus for the life I now enjoy. Did it suck when I found out my ex was cheating on me? Big time. I grieved the loss of a life I knew. I cried until my sides ached, survived on antacids, and had to apologize to more than one pillow that had the shit punched out of it. But slowly I learned to forgive him (and her) and shift my focus from how wronged I was to how I could create good for myself and others from it. This book you are reading is but one example.

Just imagine how powerful you will be over the state of your mind and life when the choices of others and circumstances around you begin to lose their power over you. This, my beautiful friend, is precisely how you begin to create and shape your world.

Look, most people are really good people. Some are assholes. Why give the latter power over you?

FAQ is how you not only release the power anger and regret hold over you, but leverage it to your benefit. FORGIVE and ASK new QUESTIONS. It's not that complicated. It really isn't. I'm not saying it's easy, but it is simple, and you can do it. It will put you in a supreme position of power. It is you, getting behind the wheel of your life again, clear in destination, the direction in your hands.

One final point I want to make on this topic. Minor bruises and mild scrapes heal on their own. Deeper cuts need a little more attention. We need to clean them out and protect them from possible infection. But there are times when our injuries are severe enough that we require some trained help. Maybe we need stitches. Maybe we need a bone reset and put in a cast. Our lives may depend on it. None of us are ashamed to go see a doctor to help "reset" a part of us so we can properly heal. The same goes for those more severe emotional wounds. It is feasible that some courageous exploring and creating new meaning can be handled on your own. It is also possible that you need a little help. A good therapist might be what you need to properly "reset" your wound so you can go about healing yourself the rest of the way. Don't be afraid or ashamed to seek out help if you feel you need it.

When you suffer, either at the hands or words of someone else, yourself, or circumstance, and you take positive, constructive action as a result, you create meaning in your life. Meaning is the new money. It raises you up, guides you, makes you stronger, and allows you to make an impact and fulfill your reason for being here. You become an alchemist as you do.

What if you accepted that your history, the sum of your experiences (both good and bad) contribute to your wholeness and strength, *not* your weakness? What if your pain is a doorway to step through to discover your purpose, fulfillment and the life you always knew *had* to be possible for you? And what if, by recognizing and knowing this, you step right into your most powerful self? The real one. The whole one. The wounded, but healed and courageous warrior. All of a sudden, you strip your past of its power and claim it as your own. It's yours for the taking. And now is the time.

Beauty Regimen

Identify something that <u>angers</u>
or <u>saddens</u> you about you, your past, or your present.
Write down three things you learned as a result.
Write down three different constructive actions you
can take to create a positive response and impact.
Act on at least one right now.

<u>Identify</u>

1. Amanda situation
2. My family's divorce
3. Trevin's deep wounds from
   the church.

<u>Result</u>

pray

1. God is going to reveal how
   he wants to use me.

keep my eyes on Him

2. I am determined not to get
   divorced - but to have a great
   family.

pray

3. I can - should - [54]believe in the
   power of prayer

4

Own Your Life

If we really love ourselves, everything in our life works.

-Louise Hay

Something you may not know about me is that I have a decent amount of experience investing in real estate. I have purchased distressed homes and renovated them for either a long-term hold and rent strategy or flip for a faster chunk of money. In some cases, I literally created income from nothing. I'd borrow enough money from a private investor to purchase, rehab and cover a year's worth of carrying costs, renovate the property creating a significantly increased value, then refinance through a bank, pay the original investor back, and rent out the property for positive cash flow. When the process is complete, I have zero money into it, and I'm making money every month. That's an infinity return on your money. Why am I telling you this? It has zero to do with bragging and everything to do with becoming your most beautiful self living your most beautiful life. You'll understand shortly.

Until now, I haven't talked about it much. My focus and purpose in life are to use my communication skills, either through writing, speaking, or radio, to empower women to see themselves in the best light, step into their power, and live happily. Whenever I mentioned in a radio interview or at a speaking engagement about the success I had as a real estate investor, the interest shifted. People wanted me to share with them my methods of profiting in real estate and lost interest in the message I was there to share about focusing on your internal set of circumstances to manifest the life you desire, not the other way around.

This happened because most people believe when you create value around you and become financially comfortable or even wealthy, you will finally feel worthy on the inside. So that's all they became interested in. But if we count on what's around us to give us the internal feelings of confidence, self-worth, peace of mind and happiness we desire, we give our power away. We make our internal state contingent on our external circumstances. Will that work sometimes? It could. But what happens if it doesn't? Enter a sense of being a powerless victim of circumstance and worse, a failure.

If money created the internal states we desire, why does

a young, talented and financially successful Demi Lovato struggle? Why would Anthony Bourdain take his own life? Why would Kate Spade, a brilliant, beautiful, admired woman who was wealthy beyond my personal comprehension choose the same? Money can make your life a heck of a lot more comfortable and fun. No doubt. And by all means, go for it! But please understand this. It is *not* the primary source of your worth. No matter how much you've accumulated, your monetary worth will never be of the highest value in your lifetime.

The most valuable asset, regardless of what your resume and balance sheet may look like, is you. The you who has found the courage to show up whole, make peace with your past, accept what cannot be changed, and transform your negative experiences, talents, skills, and wisdom into something worthy of your life and time here. *That's* how you feel confident and worthy. That's when you discover a continuous supply of courage to keep growing. That's how you create the internal state you desire and best equip yourself to create the external set of circumstances you'd prefer.

My success investing in real estate involved seeing an opportunity to increase value with a vision for what could be and sticking to it no matter the obstacles, having the courage to take some calculated risk and take action, hard work, asking for and accepting help when I needed it and hiring those more skilled than me to do what was beyond my capabilities. And the most important factor? I had to share the final product with others, either through renting or selling.

How does this tie into what I aim to do for you, your

self-esteem and sense of confidence and self-worth? You can apply a virtually identical approach to your life. It begins by crafting a vision for what the happiest, most peaceful and confident version of you looks and feels like. And you complete the process when you bring *forth* into this world what only you uniquely can.

So many of us are on a hamster wheel of trying to *get* from life and the world to feel happy and like we're enough. I'm telling you it's the reverse. Position yourself to *give* and produce the best of you, your abilities, talents, experiences, and you will be rewarded in ways beyond your wildest imagination. That may come in the form of opportunity, joy or wealth. Or all of the above.

Over the course of my time as an investor, I've rented to quite a few people. Some were and still are fantastic. They paid on time and took good care of the property. Others, not so much. I could tell you stories that would make your skin crawl. But back to the point. To a person, there is a significantly different mentality between someone who rents versus someone who owns. A person who rents may keep the place clean and well kept, but rarely does she invest in upgrading the look and value of the property. Why would she? She's just passing time there for now. She doesn't gain the reward for investing in and improving a place she rents. So status quo it is or maybe some neglect or even destructive behavior enters the picture, decreasing the value and generating the need for repair. Worn out and run down. You get where I'm going with this, right?

Are you just renting your life or will you choose to own and invest in it? Do you want to be a tenant, occupying space, passing the time? Are you passively living your life? Maybe even neglecting yourself or engaging in destructive thinking or actions? Or do you want to be an investor in you who sees what you and your life can be, hold that vision, take the necessary risks, work hard without giving up, accept help and even get professional or skilled help if you need it? Are you ready to share the unique and immeasurable value of you with the world?

Perhaps until now, you haven't seen clearly that you, your life and time here are your most valuable asset. One small shift in thinking in how you see yourself and your life can be the point of no return to catapult yourself to a new world . . . one that looks and feels on the inside and on the outside as the highest and best vision possible. This is the power you possess. This is how much capacity you have to create or reinvent yourself and your life as you wish. This is how opportunity shows up that you previously couldn't see. This moment, right here and now, could be your turning point.

Own you. Own your life. Recognize your power and *create* value. Step up. Show up as an investor in you. Appreciate your current value. Maximize your future potential. Why do many women fall short here? Because somehow, we've come to believe it's selfish, and that our value lies only in what we sacrifice for others, thereby putting ourselves last. It's total bullshit. *Make yourself and your rising up to your potential a priority.*

Now that I've got your attention and hopefully agreement, let's talk about some of the ways to do that. Your recognition alone is a massive step, an about-face. The rest is simply execution.

Start with the basics . . . the structure and foundation. That's your physical body. Quit taking it for granted, ignoring or even damaging it. You know what you need to do. So do it. Stop making excuses. You can think about, dream about, wish about all you want. What are you going to *do*? I could spend the next few pages reminding you of what is healthy, strengthens you and increases your mental capacity and energy. Would I be telling you anything you don't already know? Not likely. Do what it is you know you need to in order to take care of this priceless vessel that holds your soul. Talk about a feeling of coming home, of a renewed sense of confidence and strength. A single decision has the capacity to rock your world. Make it. Stick to it. Then allow all of the thousands of little choices that follow support that one decision.

Take better care of yourself. You don't need to shoot for perfection. There is no such thing. Let your choices and habits be dominated by what you know is good for you and allow yourself some enjoyment in between. Eat your grilled chicken salad for lunch Monday through Friday and have a martini (or even three) on Saturday.

Want to know one of the biggest sources of mental fog and headaches? Dehydration. Drink. More. Water. Walk or exercise at least four out of seven days a week. Chill for three if you want. Look to tip those scales toward what increases your health and strengthens you. Don't make it about a New Year's resolution that completely uproots your life. How successful have you been in the past dong so? Make it about a loving and compassionate decision to recognize and invest in the priceless asset that is you and let the majority of your choices support that. If you need a little bit of expert help in this area, well go search it out. Read blogs and books. Hire a nutritionist or trainer if you have the capacity and so choose. You'll never be your highest and best version of you or create the type of life you want without doing so. You don't need to make a big deal out of it. Don't make it complicated. Just decide and take the next step. And the next one.

Another crucial factor to consider relative to the health and strength of your body has to do with one of my very favorite things in the world . . . sleep. It is absolutely amazing the clarity I gain and mood I (and others) enjoy when I am well-rested. You may think that less sleep and more time doing is the most productive approach. I call bullshit on this too. Lack of sleep causes mental fog, mistakes, forgetfulness, and the universally-dreaded weight gain. It's simply not healthy. When you get solid rest, everything you do while awake is done at a higher level, including the functioning of every organ in your body. Get off the computer and electronic devices and away from the "Unreal Housewives." Create a night time routine that calms you down, clears your mind, and focuses on what you accomplished that day and what's good about you and your life. And get your ass to bed earlier.

So you now realize the importance of taking care of and investing in you. Your physical health is the foundation. What's next? What's the vision of who and how you want to be? What would the most valuable version of you look like? What will you feel like? I want you to answer these questions in writing. And I dare say the last question is the most important, as I will say it time and time again, everything around you reflects what's going on inside you. As you grow in self-love and appreciation, self-worth and self-confidence, your world has no choice but to transform and upgrade itself to align.

How else can you increase your value and worth as you move toward the higher version of you? The more you know, the more you grow. The more you grow, the more capacity you have to produce. I get we are all busy these days. Maybe you even just huffed out loud thinking *You have no idea!* We'll talk shortly on how to alleviate some of that pressure, but for now, let me ask you something. When was the last time you picked up a self-help book (prior to this one) or biography of a highly successful person? When was the last time you decided to learn something new? Whatever that may be . . . dance, graphic design, or a new language. You may have a really intense schedule, but pay attention to the time you have in your day in which you have full freedom to choose what to do, such as the time spent scrolling Facebook or Instagram or watching television. Does the time spent doing so get you closer to what you want? If not, what will? There's a good chance that new knowledge or a new skill will.

I read almost every day. It's typically the first few minutes of my day over a cup of coffee. There is so much to know about ourselves and the world we live in. Over the past few years, I have taught myself how to use Photoshop. It has allowed me to design the cover for this book, *Happy Bitch, Pink Pretty Thoughts,* and *Share This Journal.* I've created many logos for myself, friends, and charities. In the beginning, I was clueless, and through much trial and error, I am now a pro. I find this skill priceless for what I want to accomplish. You can take a class or grow your knowledge and skills through self-study. You can learn just about anything by watching YouTube videos. Whatever works for *you*. A major part of your worth lies in what you contribute, and what you contribute is based on a combination of your natural talents, skills, and knowledge.

I want you to keep a few running questions in the back of your mind going forward. *Do I have to do this? Does what I'm choosing to do right now get me further or closer to the ideal version of me and my life?* If there is a way you can start saying "No." to what doesn't serve the highest vision you have for yourself and your life, do it. Not everyone may like it. Setting boundaries is healthy and necessary and one of the most powerful actions you can take to support your vision and show self-respect. You reinforce your confidence every time you set them. By saying "No." where appropriate, you open up room to say "Yes." to something new that supports you and brings you joy and fulfillment.

I'm going to address another element here that may not be PC, but I'm keeping it real. Our physical appearance affects our mental state. Investing in what you feel makes you look better, can make you feel better. There are extremes to this, of course, but generally speaking, when you invest in and care about how you present yourself to the world around you, you communicate something deeper to yourself. It's not for the approval or admiration of others and let's face it, that reinforcement can feel great, but it's more for how you feel about how you choose to show up that day. I'm not saying we all need to run out and spend thousands on plastic surgery. If you have the means, and it does the trick for you, go for it. I'm talking about caring about your appearance and doing the best you can with what you have. A good haircut and color can do wonders.

I work from home and practically live in yoga pants, but there are times when I step it up simply because I feel better when I do. I co-host a weekly radio show alongside my fabulous gal pal Jonna Spilbor. Sometimes I show up in ripped jeans and a tank top. Other times, I sit behind a microphone in skinny jeans, five-inch, hot-pink heels, and big hoop earrings. Can the audience see me? No. I do it for how it makes me feel.

Do what you can with what you have. Don't try to mimic or be like anyone else. You sell yourself out when you do that. Do *you* to the best of your abilities. I had a great aunt who lived until eighty-seven years old. I never laid eyes on her without her hair colored and styled, earrings in her ears, and lipstick on. It was a beautiful expression of her. And maybe the most beautiful expression of you is wearing your favorite jeans, flip flops, a clean graphic tee, and a ball cap. Okay, I just described me, but you get the point.

I've saved the best investment tip for last. This little nugget is so valuable it could qualify as insider information. It has that much power to increase your worth exponentially. Your most powerful, creative and healthy state of being is happiness. Every single organ and system in your body functions optimally when you are happy.

Shawn Achor, CEO of Good Think, through research conducted at Harvard University, discovered that those who went from negative or neutral, to feeling positive, demonstrated a 31 percent increase in productivity[3]. They also increased their chances of a promotion by 40 percent. Happiness contributes to your success—big time. Success isn't the key to happiness. Happiness is the key to success. It also opens the door to creativity. Achor's research also showed that creativity and the ability to find solutions to problems jumped a whopping 300 percent when people were happier. When you feel good, you are in an optimal state for anything you want to accomplish, create, or contribute. Do you think you ought to place a little more importance on doing what makes you happy?

Think about this as well. You've heard there is a psychosomatic connection, and that stress and worry can make you sick, right? Doesn't it make sense then that the opposite is also true? Do you think it's possible that as we place a higher importance on our happiness and search out and experience what makes us happy, we can actually prevent illness or even heal ourselves? I do. I believe it 100%. Consciously looking for ways to stress less and relax more is a necessary part of maintaining your value. Think of it as mowing the lawn, cleaning out the gutters, or getting your furnace serviced. If you don't, things begin to break down and create bigger problems.

Taking care of you, making better choices regarding your physical health, emotional wellbeing, appearance, growth, and happiness all increase your value. And when your value increases, what happens? You have more to give and contribute. You simply cannot be the most powerful and beautiful version of yourself possible by putting you and your needs last. If you do, you'll end up run down, vacant, abandoned, and of no value to anyone.

When you shift your perspective and realize just how priceless you are, you open yourself to seeing what you do for yourself not as selfish, but as intelligent—not only intelligent but flat-out necessary.

Decide to invest in you. Self-appreciation and self-care is an act of love for all. The more you grow and learn, the healthier you are, the better you feel about yourself, the happier you are, the more you contribute to society and those you love, and the more you fulfill your very reason for being here. There is just no valid argument you could make to the contrary. I said it before, and I'll say it again. You came here for a reason. Treating yourself poorly is a great way to avoid fulfilling the purpose of your life and arriving at the end with regret. That may sound a bit harsh, but there couldn't be more love wrapped in these words. I want you to discover your purpose and live a fulfilling life and feel good and confident about yourself. It begins with self-appreciation and self-care.

Treat yourself better, and your life gets better.

If your current conditions, internal and/or external, are unpleasant or difficult, don't let this discourage you. Little, consistent efforts result in massive change over time. Start making a little room in your life to do what you enjoy and make you the priority you ought to be. Take baby steps. Just giving yourself permission to do so will lift your spirits and increase your sense of worth. Take a bubble bath, go for a walk in nature, flip through your favorite magazine, or meet a girlfriend for a glass of wine or cup of coffee. Depending on where you are, and I've been there (I share the story in *Happy*

Bitch,) you may need to begin by relearning what makes you
happy . . . and that's a great and beautiful place to start. As
you do more and more of what you enjoy, you send a
powerful message to yourself, to others around you, and the
universe as a whole as to your worth. I would love for you to
share with me your baby steps toward a happier you. Find
and tag me on Facebook or Instagram as @kerylpesce.

You, my friend, are worthy of everything you desire to
be, do and have. All of it. Deep down, I know you know it.

You are the only you there will ever be. Perhaps now is
the moment you begin owning that.

Beauty Regimen

Identify three things you enjoy doing that
are 100% under your control.
Act on one in the next 48 hours.

1. massage
2. getting full
   9 hrs. of sleep
3. Run

Keryl Pesce

5

Open Says Me

When things don't add up, start subtracting.

-Unknown

You're reading this book because there is something you want. What is it? Pause for a moment and think about it. This is really important. — To Connect with Nicole.

Was your answer something you feel is lacking in your life? Maybe you wish you had more money, more time, an accomplishment like landing a job, a degree, or a book you want to write, or a loving relationship. Join the club. Ask just about anyone what it is he or she needs to live a better life, and most likely the answer will involve something that person

felt was missing. The overwhelming majority of us believe
our lives will be happier, more enjoyable, and successful when
we have more . . . of whatever. Fill in the blank. And until we
get that thing, person, or experience that is missing, our lives
are lacking in some way.

As a result, what do we then do? We cram more and
more into our days, worries, and closets in search of what we
feel we need so we can finally feel accomplished, successful
and happy. Keep doing, acquiring and achieving *more*. More is
the new black. It goes with everything. Haven't you heard?

But here's the rub. Is our incessant search for more
giving us the results we desire? Have the things you've stuffed
into your mind, day or drawers helped you feel happier and
more confident? Is your world a better place as a result? Or
do you feel overwhelmed and stressed, as if your head just
might explode if one more thought pops in? Do you lack the
time to *actually enjoy* the things you worked so hard to buy and
the people you choose to share them with? All those items
you bought at the mall or on Amazon, do they now sit piled
in a corner or in the bottom of your closet creating an additional source of stress because they remind you of your lack
of time to organize and tidy up? "Someday I'll get to
organizing all this stuff I have," we tell ourselves while
simultaneously believing we are lacking, thinking "Someday
I'll have enough." We've oxymoroned ourselves into quite a
conundrum, don't you think?

What if we've got this whole thing backward? What if
what we need to feel happier, more relaxed and accomplished
actually involves less, not more? Now that's a head-scratcher.

Let's back up for a sec and talk about goals, what it is

you want. Why is it you get up every day, get dressed in whatever "uniform" suits your professional role, commute to a job that likely causes you more stress than is rewarding, and work with people you've secretly wondered how they ever landed their jobs to begin with? What is it that you want that effort and sacrifice to give you? Whatever your answer is to that, whether it's a Carnival cruise to the Bahamas, a new car, or to get out from under your debt, how do you expect you will feel when you get it? There is something super important here I want you to understand, and it's true for all of us. What you are really after isn't a material thing or accomplishment at all. *It's a feeling.* No matter your particular goals, what you are ultimately after is the feeling you expect to experience once you achieve them.

In an ironic twist of fate, in our pursuit of that which we believe will make us happy, we often times end up overworked and overwhelmed. I'm not here to tell you wanting more is a bad thing. It's normal and healthy. The problem comes in when we delay our enjoyment until we receive or achieve, living a stressful existence *now* with the hopes of this external circumstance or event showing up and making us happy. It's called giving your power away. And this book is all about claiming it back.

So how do we open up our lives for more of what we *really* want, which in the end is a good feeling state?

The operative word here is *open*.

Let's return once again to nature to understand. Have you ever gazed up at a star-filled night sky? As kids, we laid right down on the grass on summer nights to take it in, excited if we were lucky enough to catch a glimpse of a shooting star. There is something magical and awe-inspiring when we look at the millions of stars in the sky, even as adults. Let me ask you something. What is a crucial element for our ability to see and appreciate the stars and constellations? The space between the stars, right? In fact, there is significantly more space than actual stars. *It is the space where nothing exists* that allows us to appreciate what we do see. Imagine a night sky without the dark space. It would be blinding, burning light. The space *has* to exist.

Here's another way to think of it. Imagine a symphony or even your favorite song without the silence between the notes and words. There would only be unbearable noise. Imagine your day without a moment to relax . . . oh wait . . . never mind. No need to imagine. Bottom line, and in accordance with the laws of nature, the best life has to offer us cannot be enjoyed without space.

Which leads us to the question of the hour. Is it possible that achieving our goals, which we've determined are ultimately a good-feeling state, requires us to open up more room in our lives? More time in our day, more quiet between thoughts and more room in our physical spaces? All of which ultimately involve what? Less. Fewer commitments, less incessant thinking and worry, and less physical clutter. I'll take a "Hell yes!" here.

It may not be what we're accustomed to thinking, but it makes a lot of sense. So let's talk about what that might look like in your life. How can you begin opening up more space?

Let's target the easiest one first because it doesn't involve a major change in our thinking habits or time commitments, although tackling it could have a massive impact in how you feel and what actually does show up in your life–including you.

I'm talking about the physical space around you. Whether you realize it or not, there is an intimate, reciprocal relationship between your physical surroundings and your mental state. If your thoughts are cluttered, most likely the space around you is as well. And if the space around you is cluttered, it will result in cluttered thoughts and feelings.

One of the easiest, quickest and most beneficial things you can do to calm anxiety, clear your head and lift your spirits is to take some time to de-clutter. It doesn't cost you a dime, and it's something you can do right now and get immediate positive results.

It's one thing to pick up and organize what's laying around, such as clothing or mail, but true de-cluttering and the benefits it gives us isn't just about putting items in drawers, closets, or the basement where they're out of sight. Equally important is to first go through and get rid of what you no longer need, use, or love.

What you hang on to, whether you realize it or not, actually communicates with you. You are in an on-going subconscious dialogue with your stuff. The clutter is saying "Hey, I see you don't have enough time to deal with me again. Great decision-making skills you have." And each time you open the closet to get something which, by the way, you can't freaking find because it's jammed in with everything else you shoved out of sight, you agree with the clutter. "Ugh, what a mess! One of these days, I won't be under constant pressure to get things done, and I'll get to it." Or, "My head is spinning. I just can't deal with going through this shit and making one more decision today." At least you and your shit are on the same page.

But here's the thing. Neither one of you is helping each other. Your clutter is weighing you down and holding you back from the life you truly desire. And your decision not to do something about it is as well. Captain Obvious here: your clutter can't clear itself out on its own. You have to stop running from it and do something about it. You won't even offend me if you stop reading right now and put me down to go clear out your physical space. More results come from doing than thinking. I'll be right here waiting when you get back, feeling accomplished and refreshed. It's up to you.

I realize there are complete books on this topic and even de-cluttering experts you can hire, but to me, it seems pretty straightforward. It begins with recognizing the importance to our emotional well being. Then make the decision to do it. Take action. Choose a drawer, closet, room, car or even your purse. Put on some music, pour a glass of wine if you want, pull everything out and start asking the magical de-cluttering question. "Does this make me happy?" If it doesn't, put it in one of two piles – a trash pile or a donate to Goodwill pile. Then whatever is left, organize neatly.

Picture your closet right now. How do you feel when you open it? Now imagine you open your closet and all that is left, organized neatly, are things you love, things that make you happy. De-cluttering your space is a happiness-boosting project. It's a fabulous way to create a better inner and outer world for yourself.

By the way, the stuff you've decided to throw out or donate? Get rid of it. Don't leave it bagged up in the hall for a week or a month until you have the opportunity to drop it off. *Make the time.* Get it out of your space and off your mind.

In addition to physical objects creating clutter, so do unfinished projects. All of those little tasks you keep putting off for more important, pressing responsibilities actually aren't so little. Because collectively, they add up and become important. All together, it's like a crowd of hecklers shouting at you "Nah, nah, you're too busy. You aren't productive enough to take care of us!"

Here's what I suggest. Take what I like to call "a little shit day." Address all the little projects you believe aren't important that you keep waiting for enough time to do. Return that shirt that doesn't fit. Go through the pile of magazines. Wash the inside of your windshield. Return your bottles for the deposits. Take the time to address the "unimportant" tasks because collectively the little things become a big thing as a whole, and that *is* important to your well being. I do this periodically, and I feel like a million bucks when I'm done. Trust me on this. Just do it. It is one of the most productive and life-enhancing actions you can take.

Okay, on to the next de-cluttering, space-making project . . . your jammed-up, crammed-up, clogged-up mind. You know the one. It never shuts up. It's constantly carrying on about what you should do, shouldn't do, what to take care of, worry about, fix, figure out, what to be afraid of, what to beat yourself up over, what you need to do, lose or change to be accepted and loved, yadda, yadda, yadda. Obsess much? The good news is you're not alone. The bad news is you're not alone. Incessant thinking and worry is an epidemic these days. You're not a freak. You're part of the herd. You definitely fit in here. The question is do you want to?

Theoretically, you could walk from New York to LA.
But of course not without taking breaks and resting, or else
you'd break down before you reached your destination. Look
at your thinking in the same way. You can get where you
want to in life. You can shape your world. You can achieve
the internal and external states you desire. And yes, that
requires effort. Just as important, it requires rest. It requires
you to practice slowing down your thoughts and creating
space in your head. Your brain needs a break.

Practicing meditation can do wonders for your sense of
peace and happiness. If you already meditate, good for you. If
you've been thinking about it but haven't pulled the trigger,
give it a try. If, however, the thought of carving out 15-30
minutes to sit still and quiet your thoughts actually feels like
pressure, don't start there. The point of this book and everything I share is to take some weight off your shoulders, not
add. If this is you, here are some alternatives.

The first thing you can do is simply raise your awareness
of your thinking. As humans, we have this fascinating ability
to not only think, but to also *observe* our thinking. Make the
decision to raise your awareness of the types, quantity, and
speed of your thinking. Step into the role of the observer.
And as the observer, and also the driver, you can choose to
slow your thoughts down. When you feel stressed and overwhelmed, I guarantee your thoughts are traveling through
your head at a high rate of speed. Slow down. As you do, you
will gain in clarity and calmness. That's a promise.

The other way you create space in your thinking without
needing to carve out time to meditate is to do mini, 60-

second meditations. Don't tell me you don't have 60 seconds. Bull. In one-minute increments, as often as you choose throughout the day, focus on your breathing. Take your thoughts off of what you need to figure out or do and put them on your breath. It's like taking a break and giving your mind a delicious and healthy little snack.

Perhaps the most powerful benefit of slowing down and creating space between your thoughts is this—it is the only way you will tap into the wisdom of your intuition. And I'm telling you right now, that bitch is brilliant. It's like you have the great and powerful Oz available with the tap of your pretty little slippers. Intuition is one of the most amazing gifts we've been given. It's always available and always right. Our job is to remember it's there, quiet down, ask, listen, and trust in the guidance. Sometimes that comes as a feeling, not even a thought. It shows up to you as a sense to call someone, turn down a certain street, or say no. You've had gut feelings. Whether you listened or not, when you reflect on it, your gut feeling was leading you in the right direction. It's like our inner compass. We need to practice tuning in. That can only happen when we deliberately quiet our thinking and listen.

At the risk of this freaking you out a bit, it is a well-documented, scientific fact that the cells throughout your body hold memories. They contain information and knowledge. There are countless cases of people who are the recipients of organ transplants who take on new character-istics and preferences. People suddenly start craving a food they've never liked in their lifetime or start listening to music they never cared for. They sometimes call forth very specific information about their donors. Your brain is not the only part of you that thinks, holds memories or contains wisdom. Your entire body does. Take care of it. Settle down your thoughts and open the doorway to your body of knowledge.

There is something else important I want you to consider. Sometimes one of the most intelligent and productive approaches to a problem is to temporarily let go of it. Putting some space between you and the problem or challenge opens up a gap for wisdom to show up. I can't tell you how many times I've been trying to figure something out and grow frustrated in the process. Guess what happens when we get aggravated? Our mental capacity shrinks. I realize letting go isn't always the easy thing to do, but there are times it is the smartest thing you can do. Go for a walk, get a drink of water, step away and do something that takes mild effort. And when you least expect it, the answer and solution you were striving so hard to figure out pops in your head without effort. You've probably already experienced this accidentally. Now you have a mechanism you can deliberately employ to help you.

Along these lines (you can tap into the above to clean this clutter,) are the open loops in your life. Unmade decisions are mental clutter. They could be minor, such as the piles of items on your stairs going to the second floor that you haven't grabbed because you are unsure of where to put them (guilty) or major life decisions about what direction to go. Start closing some loops. Make decisions. Not every one may be correct. No one on planet earth ever has or will get through his or her lifetime without making a "wrong" decision. I use quotes because sometimes what initially appears wrong ends up leading us down an amazing path we

Need to do.

never saw coming.

The final area of space I want to talk with you about is the demands on your time and attention. Are most of your days a blur? Do you lay your head down at night, exhausted, wondering just where another day went? Do you feel a bit like a pinball getting whacked around all day by obligations, deadlines, and responsibilities? Do you long for a few minutes, an hour, or a whole day to just do what *you* want to do? Has it been more than a little while since you did? Sister, I realize this isn't easy for us women, but we need to treat ourselves, our desires and dreams as a high priority. We need time in our lives to just be, to do what makes us happy, to relax and unwind. It's not selfish. It's healthy. It's soul soothing. It sets you up to contribute even more than you do without it.

I realize you may have a decent amount of obligations you can't just walk away from. But where in your life can you begin saying no? I mentioned in a previous chapter. There are times when "No." is a big fat "YES!" Boundaries are healthy. They build confidence and self-respect and command respect from others. Setting boundaries is an exercise in self-love. Imagine creating a life that is built on saying "No." to what you don't want and what no longer serves you and saying "Yes." to what makes you happy.

Just like the exercise we did with your closet. Imagine what your life will look like when this becomes a regular process you apply to living your life as a whole, and what is left, is dominated by what brings you joy. Wow! That's the kind of life we all want. Here's the key. Deciding what to say no to and carve out of your life only becomes possible when you are clear on what it is you *do* want. Revisit the last chapter if need be.

What's truly powerful about understanding and practicing opening up and creating more space in your life is that it is a universal principle. What that means is you may decide to clean out your closet or your physical space, and through that opening up, something you've wanted shows up elsewhere in your life. My husband and I, after over a decade of saying we would do it, took 90 minutes, two Saturdays in a row to clean out our basement. We did exactly what I suggested above. Shortly after, I received a phone call from a friend of mine whose friend was selling his home. He thought of me first to buy it as an investment. I purchased it and expect to profit over $30,000. Perhaps that opportunity coming my way had nothing to do with our decision to clean out and make room in our basement, but guess what? My gut tells me the two were directly connected.

There's something else I want you to understand if it hasn't already occurred to you as a result of this discussion, and it is perhaps the kingpin concept of this chapter. What makes you beautiful is far more about what is unseen about you than what is seen. It's not about the color or smoothness of your skin, the size and shape of your body, or any physical attribute. It's about the energy of your presence. You radiate beauty when you open yourself to seeing yourself (your *whole* self,) others, and all situations through the eyes of compassion. It is a powerful choice which allows you to show up to yourself and others as the most beautiful version of you there is . . . one that is grounded in love. It's pure, never fades, and is available to all of us equally in every moment of every day.

    Make no mistake. It is your inner presence, that which we cannot see with our eyes, which allows your true beauty to shine. That is the truth of who you are.

Beauty Regimen

Clean something out in the next 24 hours.
Choose a junk drawer, dresser, or closet.
Bring whatever is donation-worthy to your
local Goodwill or Salvation Army.
Throw out the rest.

6

Demote Fear,
Promote Courage

The secret to happiness is freedom...
And the secret to freedom is courage.

-Thucydides

We've talked about how important it is to your health, happiness, and well being to give yourself space and permission to feel "negative" emotions. In doing so, you take the pressure of judgment off of yourself and allow the emotion to be expressed and therefore move through and out of you. As you now know, the irony is that by *not* immediately trying to suppress negative emotions at all costs, you actually lessen

83

their intensity and impact. Your allowance rather than denial removes the power from the emotion itself and puts it in your hands. I'm going to offer up a bit of an exception to this "Rule of Building a Powerful You" and that has to do with fear.

I still recommend that you allow space to experience all emotions, but a word (or 3,000) of advice when it comes to fear as it's a bit stickier than the others. You can be angry and still move forward with your day and life. You can be sad and still show up. But fear? That baby can shrink you to a shadow of your true self. And it's sneaky because it can be subtle. It can show up as not voicing which restaurant you really prefer to go to or what movie you want to watch for fear of disappointing others. One instant of remaining quiet to what it is you want in and of itself isn't such a big deal. But if it becomes your default mode, you're compromising your integrity. You are not being honest, and you communicate to yourself and those around you that what you want doesn't matter. It does matter. Remember, integrity is integration, wholeness. It is your truth. Regularly not voicing your preferences atrophies both your courage muscle and sense of self-worth. Then you wake up one day wondering why no one gives a shit about what you want and want makes you happy. That never happens, does it?

I'm a big "Why?" person. I like to know why we do the things we do and think the way we think. So let's begin there. Let's explore what it is we really fear and why. Then we'll get into how to adjust the role it plays in your life so it protects you from harm, but doesn't hold you back from stepping into your parallel universe and living a full life.

It's been said that the number one fear is fear of public speaking, and that some fear it more than death. I'm not so sure about that, but it definitely ranks pretty high on the totem pole. If you ask me, it goes deeper than public speaking. It isn't the public speaking people are afraid of. It's being negatively judged by others that we fear. That's what we are really afraid of. And why do we fear that so much? Why do we allow the fear of how others will perceive us drive our decisions and actions? You can blame your ancestors for this one.

There was a time in human history that if we were not accepted by the tribe, there was a high likelihood it would mean certain death. If the tribe ostracized you and sent you off into the wilderness, you and you alone would be solely responsible for finding food, water, safe shelter, and fending off saber-toothed tigers or any number of other wild animals looking at you for their next meal. You literally and figuratively would become toast. So that fear of judgment of you by others? It's a survival mechanism. At the source, it's intended to keep you alive, because thousands of years ago, being part of a tribe greatly increased your chances of survival.

So understand, the root of fear is designed to keep you safe and alive. Fear has a valid job to do. We need to understand the positive role it plays but maintain awareness in our daily lives if playing by its terms (typically hiding, staying quiet, and playing small) are truly what is good for us. We need to check in with ourselves, with our fear, stay in touch with what matters to us and develop the courage to choose what is important over what scares us.

This is why we fear being rejected so much. Thousands

of years ago, rejection was life-threatening. Newsflash . . . in today's world, not being accepted ain't gonna kill you. I dare say one of the most dangerous things you can do is live your life trying to be accepted by everyone, for you risk losing your sense of self. You keep adjusting yourself to fit in and be accepted and one day you wonder why you feel so lost in your own life.

This book is about you finding your way back to you and that sense of being in the right skin and life. In the last chapter, we talked about how part of the code to unlocking the life you want to live involves less. I'll give you something else you can remove from your life to bring you more of what you want . . . lose the desire and worry to fit in. Trying to fit in is changing who you are to be accepted by those who see the world differently than you. Take the focus off of trying to fit in and on to being the true and authentic you. Guess what happens as a result? The right tribe will find you or you, it. You will naturally attract to you those who appreciate the whole and real you. I'll take a handful of people who get me over a hundred thousand "followers" who have subscribed to an image I portray.

Our upbringing is another source of our adult fears. We are raised to be good little girls, to be polite, and not do or say anything that hurts the feelings of others. All of this is great so long as we balance this with remaining true to ourselves, with what matters to us, with allowing the full expression of who we are and what we want to experience in this lifetime. The fact is though, most of us don't. I'm not suggesting you not care how your actions affect others. Of course, consider it, but begin shifting the balance of power in your life to give equal or greater merit to what *you* want.

Some believe it's a simple matter of choosing to "Be fearless." I disagree. Fear is a valid aspect of being human, so trying to banish it completely is never going to happen. It's more about deciding what role it will play in your life. It's about building a healthy relationship with this aspect of yourself.

Another one of my favorite quotes is "Courage is not the absence of fear, but rather the judgment that something else is more important than one's fear." by Ambrose Redmoon. We all experience fear. It's just that some of us have developed the courage to act in the face of it because we know that what we want and what is good for us long term is more important. So let's talk about how to build your courage rather than banishing your fears. Let's talk about how to build a healthy relationship with fear and then some specific ways to start flexing your courage muscle.

Much like we discussed in an earlier chapter, the first step I encourage you to take is to acknowledge your Fear when it shows up. When Fear pops up, allow space for it. Just as with all other aspects of you, I recommend having a conversation with it. Be curious with it. Ask it why it's showing up, what it wants for you and how it wants to help. And if it is standing in the way of something you know is important to you, politely ask it to refrain from voting on this issue. "I hear you. Thank you. Please abstain from voting."

We discussed how we banish aspects of ourselves, and how that fragments and weakens us. With fear, however, the problem is the exact opposite. We haven't banished it. We've allowed it to sit at the head of the table, making most of the decisions for us. We've allowed Fear to play too great a role. You want to find and experience the amazing sense of freedom that comes with being the true, whole, and authentic you? Adjusting the role Fear plays in your life is a pre-requisite. So let's put Fear in its place. Allow it a seat at the table. Just stop letting it be the boss of you. It isn't. *You* are the boss of you.

Demote Fear. Promote Courage.

"Fear, thank you for all you've done to keep me safe. Please sit over here on the side for now. Courage is going to take the lead for a while. If you've got something to say, speak up, but please understand from this point forward, you are *not* in charge. Courage is." It's a singular decision. Who do you want running your show?

Pause for a moment and imagine how you would show up each day with Courage in the lead role? You already possess it. It's within you. What if it's less about building it up and more about *allowing it to emerge,* allowing it to play a greater role in your decisions and direction in life?

Moving Fear from the head of the table to another seat and letting Courage take the lead is ultimately is about learning to trust yourself. It is about reinforcing to yourself that you can handle what comes your way. Even if the choices you make or actions you take don't work out as you had hoped. You trust that you can handle that too.

Fear, once our board member intended to keep us alive has taken on a new job. We need to heed its warnings when our lives truly are in danger, but most times our safety really isn't at stake. And taken to an extreme, Fear, in a very real sense, if allowed to primarily drive our decisions, ironically can be the very thing that *does* put our lives in danger.

A woman feels a lump in her breast, fears its cancer and is so afraid to hear the word, puts off going to get tested. She does so long enough that by the time she has no choice but to go, her likelihood of successful treatment is small.

Heart disease is the number one killer of women. Most cases involve advance signs, but she's afraid of knowing, afraid of what the doctor will tell her, of needing surgery, that she puts off going to get checked. She dies of a heart attack. How effective was Fear in keeping her safe? I realize these are extreme examples. And yet they happen every day. If you have a feeling something is wrong and are afraid of what you may find out, find your Courage. Go find out. Address it. Now.

If this conversation strikes a nerve with you, and you are aware that you've allowed Fear to play the role of Chair of the Board, that's a good thing. Awareness is the beginning. It's time to start flexing your courage muscles. As with any new workout, you need to build up your strength. No one joins a gym for the first time and expects to bench press 300 pounds. But many are able to do so after starting small and with repetition and steady increases, they work themselves up. Your Courage operates the same way. I'm not suggesting you close this book and go take a major step in the face of Fear (unless, of course, it involves your health.) Don't start there, because if you are in a fragile state and at the early stages of becoming whole again, your actions not working out could put you three steps back. Start small and work your way up.

Begin by speaking up when you have a simple prefer-ence. When a friend or relative asks you where you want to go to eat, say it. If your spouse gets up from the table every night without putting his plate in the sink and sits on his ass on the couch while you clean up, speak up. Don't be a douche about it. Ask politely and with respect. "Hey, I get you're tired. So am I. Going forward, can you help me out by bringing your plate over to the sink?"

If there is one thing we women are notorious for, it's expecting our mates to know what we're thinking. Shit, half the time I don't even know what I'm thinking. How can I expect my husband to know? Find your voice. Express what it is you want. Not doing so is choosing to be liked rather than respected. You may get rejected by someone else if you start saying "No," and setting boundaries, but *not* doing so is rejecting *you* and what you want.

There are times to express what you want and times to give space to those in your life to do the same. Compromise, especially for those we love, is necessary for healthy relationships. It's about balance.

Are there legitimate situations, people, and experiences worthy of our fear? Yes. Being cautious is wise. But being fearful is about not moving forward, not setting boundaries, not voicing what you want and what you don't want, not allowing your creativity to flow, not taking risks, not growing, not experiencing a full life, not allowing the full expression of all that is you. It's a big fat "No!" to life. Start saying "Yes!"

Courage is a practiced skill. Each of us has the ability to increase our capacity to be courageous. Your strength of courage will naturally increase as some of what we have already talked about helps you become whole again. As you understand and adopt what we talk about in this book, the courage within you takes a seat at the table. It begins to show up and play a role in your decisions . . . little and major.

Another way to stretch your courage is when you're out in public, strike up a conversation with a stranger . . . safely of course. The next time you're in line at the coffee shop, comment to a person near you about something he or she is wearing. In line at the grocery store and see the person behind you with something you like to cook? Say something. Open up. Each time you flex your courage muscle, even a little bit, your courage expands and your fear shrinks.

Practice getting over your fear of making mistakes. It keeps you from trying anything new. It keeps you from developing your talents and unleashing your potential. Try something new. When you do make a mistake, and you will, congratulate yourself for trying. Mistakes do not equal failure. Mistakes are growing pains. They're a sign you're expanding.

All decisions are the right decisions if your intention behind them is to grow and move you closer to the life you want to live. You either get the outcome you desire or you learn. That's a win-win.

Feeling fear is okay. It's normal. Fear is a sign of growth. Smile at it. It's not about fighting to remove Fear. It's about deciding what role it will play and building a better relationship with it.

If Fear is always in charge, you will live a small existence. You will never feel fully alive and live a rich, rewarding, exciting, and fulfilling life. Don't allow it to limit the full and true expression of you.

There's something else on this topic that is important for you to understand. Living in fear of pain doesn't prevent it, it fosters it. The discovery of my ex's affair and subsequent divorce was immensely painful. I don't ever want to experience that kind of pain again. Yet I chose to put the experience of loving again as a higher priority as I recovered and moved forward with my life. The Fear was there. I chose not to let it drive my bus. I allowed myself to fall fully in love. There is so much I would be missing out on today if I had allowed Fear to be in charge. Should it have a voice? Yes. Be in charge? No. What are you missing in the form of accomplishments, experiences, and relationships, by allowing Fear to steer you? How much pain is it causing because you're living a smaller existence than that which you were intended for and you know it?

I believe most of us know what to do to live the life we desire but are waiting to not feel afraid to do it. Flip that around. Do it anyway. Now. And *then* Fear steps aside. You've thought about what you want and need to do. Stop thinking about it and act. Thinking is mental jail. Action is freedom.

As you expand in courage, your life does as well . . . in the form of new experiences, skills, people, and opportunity. As you stretch, you create a new and larger comfort zone.

I have had a longing to be a publisher of books by or for women for a long time. For whatever reason, friends and even strangers keep coming to me for advice. And I give it every time. I love it! I believe each of us, especially women, have a book in us. So I jumped at the chance to help those who came to me. Some I guided with advice. Others I dove in, elbow deep and made it happen. The joy I feel when a woman holds her book for the first time and I know I played a part in making that happen? For me, it just doesn't get any better than that. When she goes, her story goes with her. Her unique experiences, interpretations, perspectives, once captured in a book, outlive her. Between my own books and those I helped others create and publish, I've played a part in eight books that will forever capture a piece of each woman. I did it because I believed in what I was doing and felt it was important, but never as a paid profession.

So I had the idea to become a publisher. But I kept hesitating. The reality is that the publishing space is *very* crowded. Who am I? How would I break in? Get clients? I even designed a logo for Little Pink Press and put it on my dream board. But I didn't know how to make it happen, so I waited and waited. Fear was at the helm. Then one day I decided it was time for Courage to show up and announced my services as a publisher on Facebook. Within the first month, I had my first referral . . . an extraordinary woman named Anita Vlismas. She was 80 years old, had just completed her second round of chemo and had a memoir she wanted to publish. I am thrilled I was in a position to do this for her. And it *never* would have happened if I didn't have the courage to put myself out there. At least not for me it wouldn't. And who knows? What if no other publisher picked her up? She may leave this earth having never told her story. No one else could tell it but her. And believe me, it's a lively, brave, and adventurous one. I have learned so much about living a full life from her courage and ability to embrace uncertainty. Her book may not be a self-help book on overcoming fear, but it's a powerful tool to help you do just that. Pick up and read *Beyond the Mountain*. You will be inspired and grow in courage just by reading her story.

Take a lesson from Anita. Practice allowing room for a little uncertainty in your life. Create a new mantra: "I've got this." No matter the outcome.

There's something else I want you to be aware of when it comes to fear. Pay attention to how you might be imposing your fears on those you love. Give them the latitude to grow and expand as well. Constantly maneuvering to protect someone else, especially a child, renders them unskilled at thinking for themselves and ill-equipped to overcome challenges. Sometimes the best and most loving thing you can do is *not* protect them from upset. Keep them safe from real harm? Yes, always. But acting from fear they will fail or make mistakes sets them up for pretty much certain failure and definitely anxiety and self-esteem issues. Communicate via not hovering, that you're confident in their intelligence and ability to make decisions and handle what comes their way. Try this one "You'll figure it out." Support, don't fix.

Your fear was originally designed to keep you safe and part of the tribe. Today, your comfort zone can become your danger zone. Everything you want is on the other side of fear. Your fear keeps you small. It stands in between who and where you are now and who and where you want to be.

Put measures in place if your safety truly is at risk. And where it isn't, make a decision. Take action. Nothing changes until you do. Stop hesitating. Start acting. Start moving. Start somewhere. Just start!

One more point I want to make here is to yes, take action and move forward despite your fears, but also practice patience as you do. Pushing too hard and being too impatient contains a strong undercurrent of fear. Act now and then practice patience as you move forward. Doing so implies faith and trust in yourself and the world you live in.

Beauty Regimen

Write the following in a journal:
"If I were to allow Courage to take the lead today,
I would _____." Fill in the blank.
Maybe this even becomes
how you start each day.

Keryl Pesce

7

Positive Possibilities

*When the Universe starts lining things up for you in
a way that no human mind could ever do,
it will take your breath away.*

-Rhonda Byrne

I'm going to share something that is a bit weird about me. Well, I used to think it was weird, like some sort of flaw in my personality and a lack of ability to be disciplined. Try as I might, countless gurus telling me that I need to, I suck at goal setting. Not only do I suck at it. I can't stand it. But yet we're repeatedly told we need to set measurable, specific goals with a deadline. Blech! The more structured and rigid something is, the more I avoid it. And I won't argue that perhaps I might be able to accomplish more if I did set specific goals, but the fact of the matter is and owning all that is me, I'm just not wired for it. Maybe it works for some people, but it does not inspire or motivate me.

This in itself may not fully qualify as weird, but what may, is that despite my aversion to measurable goal setting, I believe in dreaming big. Don't set a goal, but dream big? Seems a little contradictory, doesn't it? But maybe not so much. Let's explore this a bit.

I believe everything begins in thought. Anything we achieve, acquire, accomplish or feel first begins as an idea. It didn't exist, except for in our minds, and now it does. It's a bit of a magical power if you ask me. We'll get into some mind-blowing science to back that up in a bit.

In order for us to step into our fullness, our authentic, true and powerful selves, to shape who we are and how we show up, we need to have the idea first of what that will look and feel like. And in order for us to create the experiences, material items, and relationships we desire, we need to first have an idea of what those would be as well.

So there needs to be a certain amount of future projecting. Doesn't that sound more inviting than goal setting?

Let's talk about you first. Then we'll talk about what's going on around you. Feel free to write your answers out if you like.

If you projected a desired future you, what would that look like? What would you feel like? What abilities and attributes would you possess? Think about the aspects of your physical self you can affect. Have you lost weight because you've chosen a healthier approach to eating? Are you stronger and more fit because you've found the discipline to exercise? Imagine the future you standing in front of a mirror and you feel good and proud. What do you see?

What knowledge, ability or skill do you wish you had? How would you feel possessing it?

Here's a big one. How do you wish you felt about yourself? Do you want to feel calm, confident, grounded, and/or happy?

Once you've given some thought to the above and now that you have an idea of the target you're shooting for, start creating paths to it. Start asking "How?" and "What if?" Here are some examples:

-How can I create a work out schedule I will stick to?

-How can I get exercise in a way I actually enjoy?

-What if I went swimming at the local Y?

-What if I tried kayaking?

-What if I enlisted a gal pal to do this with me?

-What if I took some yoga classes?

-How can I adjust my typical daily eating habits to create a healthier, more vibrant me?

-What if I cooked on the weekend, making enough healthy food for the week?

-What if I brought four bottles of water to work each day and made sure I drank them?

Allow me to pause here and let you in on a little secret. No matter our individual desires, a common one we hold is to feel good about who we are. As you begin taking consistent action toward something you desire, move over self doubt because self pride and confidence just walked in. Let's continue.

-How can I start making more room in my life to actually do what I enjoy and do so without guilt?
-How can I show more self respect and self love so I attract more of it from others?
-What if I started setting boundaries and said "No." more often to what I don't want and got clear on what I do want?
-What if I found the courage to pursue what in my heart I know I want to do and experience . . . even if others don't approve?

By the way, I'm not talking about deliberately ignoring how your actions will affect those you love. You gotta consider that. The key is that your decisions and actions come from a place of self respect and love *along with* consideration for others who matter in your life. Make your self respect and self love the priority. You don't act absent of consideration for others, and you don't hold yourself back because you make what others expect of you your primary consideration.

-What do I wish I knew how to do?
-What skills would I like to possess?
-How can I learn?
-What if I began watching YouTube videos on my lunch hour?
-What if I took an online course?
-What if I ordered a new book from Amazon?

-What if I reached out to someone and asked her to teach me or show me how to do something?

Important to note here. Don't make your goals about the actions of other people. Don't make your dreams and aspirations dependent on the choices, preferences, and actions of another. Bring it home. Bring it to you. What can *you* do? What do you want to experience or feel?

For example, say there is someone you have strong feelings for. Maybe it's an ex, or soon-to-be-ex, or someone in a relationship with someone else, and all you think about day and night is how happy you would be if he chose you. Your heart aches. You feel powerless and hopeless for a happy existence unless he does. I'm not judging. Been there. Did that like professional following the discovery of my ex's affair. But if you ask a series of why and how questions, you'll uncover the root of what it is you really want.

Why do I want him to choose me? You may answer "Because I love him." And if he does choose me, how will that make me feel? "Happy, loved, and content." So understand what you are really after is feeling happy, loved, and content. You've just decided this person choosing you is the only way to get it. So what if you opened the door to more ways of feeling this way? If what you want is to feel happy, loved, and content, what are additional ways you might experience this?

You've got your creative juices going. You've got a better idea of what you *do* want in your life. You're opening paths to achieving what it is you desire without a rigid step-by-step plan. You may even feel a twinge of relief or excitement you haven't felt in a while. Now let's talk about why opening paths and feeling excited as you move forward versus having a rigid plan is important.

In 1937, Napolean Hill wrote the classic book *Think and Grow Rich*[4]. At the time of its release and for the many decades that have followed, the premise of the power of our thoughts to affect our outcomes was considered by most to be a theory. A few considered it bunk. Some still do today. Fast forward to modern day and a field of science known as quantum physics, what was once thought to be impossible and not capable of being proven, is now both.

Brilliant people like Einstein introduced the theory behind modern-day quantum physics in the early 1900's before Hill's book came out, but it wasn't until more recently, that the legitimacy and impact of the science has become more widely known and accepted. The field of quantum physics or quantum mechanics is essentially the behavior of matter and how it interacts with energy on the smallest of scales—that of atoms and subatomic particles. Today quantum physicists are winning Nobel Prizes for their research and discoveries. Before I bore you any further or attempt to sound like I've got the entire field of science fully understood (nope, I don't,) what is the significance to you? Why should you care?

Because we now know that at the most elemental core of all existence on planet earth and the universe exists energy. Including you. Including your thoughts. Including your feelings. Energy that communicates with, affects, and even alters what you see as solid physical matter.

I know. "You're losing me Keryl."

Get this: what you think and feel communicates with and

affects physical matter around you, other people, and every cell in your body. You're a walking wizard and don't even know it.

Has someone ever walked in a room and you had a bad feeling about him without even speaking to him? Some people will tell you you're being judgmental. I'm here to tell you that you are reading his energy. Have you ever been in a really bad mood and a bubbly person comes along and you find it annoying? Major energetic mismatch happening. It's like when you try putting two magnets together and they physically repel each other.

Have you heard of a Japanese researcher by the name of Masaru Emoto? He conducted experiments with water to demonstrate human consciousness affects the structure of water. He gathered water from a single source, put it in multiple containers and among other things, put certain words on the containers. He then froze the water, put it under a microscope, and photographed it. In one example, he put on the container the words "love and gratitude." On another, "You make me sick. I will kill you." If you're up for getting your mind blown, Google it and look at the pictures. The first photo was perfect, beautiful and resembled a snow flake. The second was discolored and distorted. In his New York Times best selling book *The Hidden Messages in Water*[5], he documents with photos many of the experiments he conducted.

If you want your own proof to experience this for yourself, pick up a book called *E-Squared – Nine Do-It-Yourself Energy Experiments that Prove Your Thoughts Create Your Reality*[6] by Pam Grout. She makes this field of study easy to understand and apply to our every day lives and offers experiments you can try out to prove to yourself the validity. One of the experiments she suggests, which I've done live more times than I can count (perhaps I can for you some day,) involves bending two wire hangers to create wands of sorts, sliding on a half of a plastic straw to act as a handle on each and watching how they move on their own, *directed ONLY by your corresponding thoughts and feelings.* I always bring up a volunteer to show it's not me manipulating the wands. The wands are held with arms extended in front of the person. As the person thinks angry or fearful thoughts, the wands drift in . . . sometimes as far as to touch each other. As the person thinks loving or kind thoughts, the wands drift out and open. I also do an experiment where I demonstrate the human body becomes physically stronger when thinking and feeling positively.

Setting rigid goals creates a pass or fail situation. The minute you start out, there is an underlying current of anxiousness, because behind the scenes, you've got a conversation going on in your head "This better happen. I have to make this happen. What if it doesn't work?" As a result, your creativity lessens and your body physically weakens.

Conversely, having a positive possibility in mind as you move toward it with a sense of openness doesn't. It allows for flow, for multiple possibilities . . . some perhaps greater and more magnificent than you can conceive.

Your thoughts and feelings are powerful. You already possess the creative force of imagination. You already use it. The challenge for many people is they use it with an undercurrent of fear and worry. Many of us use the powerful question of "What if?" to our detriment, to what could go wrong. Knowing what you now know about quantum physics and the affect you have on the world around you, this could be the very reason you are in a rut, in a reality you dislike, wondering when your break will come . . . if ever. *You* are that break. You are the power and creator of your reality. You already know how to imagine something that hasn't happened. You've been doing it your whole life. You don't need to be given new powers and strength. It's yours already. You simply need to train yourself to imagine what you want, not what you don't want, what could go right, not wrong, success (however that looks to you,) not failure.

Don't beat yourself up or freak out if you do worry or have negative thoughts. Welcome to humanity. One of the first things we talked about was allowing yourself to experience all emotions. The point is to not dwell in the negative realm, but to have your thoughts dominated by the positive possibilities. Remember, you're not failing at being you or failing at life because you have a negative thought. Let it flow through you and then gently move yourself in a better direction.

I get that what I'm suggesting may not be what you are used to hearing. But if the advice you're used to getting isn't working, maybe it's not the right approach for you. Some people are wired for hard and fast goals, and if that's been working for you, fantastic.

Dream big. Ask "What if?" questions. Let your imagination run wild. Then *detach* from the outcome. Work towards it. Take action. Stay focused and determined. That's all good stuff. But move forward with a sense of faith and openness. Accept that you may not get exactly what you're after, but the positive possibility exists that you'll get something greater or even more valuable than you first hoped for.

My good friend intuitive medium Deborah Hanlon just released her first book *In the Presence of Proof.* She was overjoyed and proud of her accomplishment, and she has such a sense of inner peace as she keeps telling me "I have no attachment to how things will play out." She's promoting it. She's talking about it and posting about it. So she is doing the work, but the work comes without pressure of results. Her joy and excitement is right here and now. She doesn't need a certain number of sales or level of ranking for her happiness. It's already here.

Speaking of enjoying the process, consider scheduling a "What if?" or "Dream big." girl's night. Gather your besties and do this with them. Go around the table and start dreaming big together. There's even more power when people of like mind gather together. They will have ideas you haven't thought of. I guarantee it. Plus, you will feel even better and more inspired because you are there to help them dream big as well.

It's not what you achieve. It's *how* you achieve. Reach for the stars. Do all you can to love and enjoy the pursuit of what you desire. *That's* the part that you get to influence and control. As much as we humans would like to believe it, we are not in control of outcomes.

Keep asking yourself "How can I enjoy the process? How can I do my best and let go of the rest?" This is a major shift in thinking that will have a massive effect on the use of the power already within you. It's as if you have a huge power plant within you, but when you make your happiness dependent on the outcome, it lies dormant.

When we get too wadded up as to exactly how things will play out, the ride is less fun, anxiety goes up, creativity goes down, and the likelihood of us achieving what we desire diminishes. Loosen up, and you will amp up and level up. Relax. Show yourself and the universe some faith. Let the power of this connected web we live in take over. Then watch the magic happen.

Beauty Regimen

Think about something that would make
you happy if you achieved it. Hold right now by yourself, or
schedule within the next seven days
with people who love and support you, a
Positive Possibilities session.
Get creative. Choose to have fun with it.
Keep asking "What if?" with positive
expectations until something
strikes you that excites you.
Then act on it.

8

Unfollow the Bullshit

*Respect yourself enough to say — I deserve inner peace —
and walk away from people and things that prevent
you from attaining it.*

— Jerico Silvers

You're finding the courage to show up whole, to not fear your sadness or anger, to not resent but *use* what has happened to you, to see and invest in the value of you, to recognize that what you may need most is less, and in doing so, you're beginning to experience your life as you are meant to. By now, I hope you are starting to settle down a bit and feel the amazing thing that is known as inner peace. Make no mistake. Your beauty shines on the outside when you are at peace on the inside.

Next let's talk about how to further influence and protect you in that state and preserve your power for what matters most to you.

Let's go back to you again, to the power you hold. So many of us make the mistake of living life less than we are worthy and capable of by not recognizing the power we have to choose how we view and respond to the world around us. You now know that I believe when change is desired, the starting point is always you . . . that you are the creator of your reality and life. What I want to talk about here is that although this is true, that your outer world is a reflection of your inner views and inner world, your outer world *does* influence how you use your power. Much like we discussed how physical clutter affects your mental clutter and vice versa, there is a reciprocal relationship between the world within and the world without.

If you remember one idea from this book, please make it this one . . . your inner peace, self confidence and happiness are your buried treasures. When you experience these, anything, and I mean *anything*, is possible. You step into the realm of miracles. Sister, listen to me here. You *gotta* protect that shit! You can look at it, marvel at its beauty and worth, but *do not* let others get their hands on it. Guard it like you would the life of your child or pet. Protect. Your. Peace.

Let's talk about how to do that.

Bottom line, you need to unfollow the bullshit. You need to recognize who and what enhances how you feel and who and what doesn't. And then take measures to eliminate or at least limit your exposure to what doesn't enhance your sense of happiness and self confidence.

Let's start with who. You're got roughly 16 hours a day of being awake. For many people who have trouble sleeping, it's a lot more. In your waking hours, who is there with you? How do you feel when you are around them? Inspired or self conscious? Comfortable and at peace or like you're walking on egg shells? Happy and silly or serious and stressed? Do you feel like you need to mask or alter aspects of yourself or do you feel free to be authentic?

Do an inventory of who gets time in your life on a regular or every day basis and ask yourself these questions. It's important that you understand I'm not talking about someone you care about who is going through a difficult time. We need to support the people we love. I'm talking about people who regularly influence you toward the negative aspects just mentioned . . . the dreaded energy vampires.

Do you see a pattern? Do you see something perhaps you haven't wanted to admit or recognize? The fact is you may need to make some changes in the people you surround yourself with. People who regularly make you feel worse about yourself are out-right thieves. They're stealing that which is of most value to you, and it's up to you to protect yourself from them. Now admittedly, some might be easier to avoid than others, but your first step no matter what is to realize how important this is.

The remedy may involve not giving this person your time and attention anymore. You don't have to be mean or hurtful about it. That doesn't help anyone in any situation. This is a vote for you, not against another. And if that seems too harsh and doesn't sit well with you, well my friend, it's about time you start setting some boundaries and finding your voice. Don't assume others know how they affect you. Many of us women have been brought up to be good little girls, overly polite and to put the feelings of others above our own . . . always . . . and it doesn't serve us!

Do you remember how a DJ posing in a picture with Taylor Swift reached under the back of her skirt and grabbed her ass? In a follow up interview, she mentioned how angry she was at herself for thanking him for coming as she does to all others. It's understandable. She was in shock. She had just been sexually assaulted. But look at the power of our upbringing, where girls are supposed to be polite. The good news is she ended up winning a lawsuit against him. She killed it in her testimony. You want to see a smart and confident female who has found her voice? Check out her responses during the trial. You will be inspired. No doubt about it.

If someone is devaluing you by lowering your self esteem or disrupting your inner peace, speak up and address it or remove them from your life. Or both. I realize in some cases it is easier than others. If it's a casual friend, you can stop spending time with her. Not too difficult. In some cases it may be family. Here's where a little judgment is required. You need to ask yourself how you can reduce this person's exposure to and affect on you and keep the peace in the larger scheme of things. You don't want to upset your entire family dynamic if you don't have to, although you may need to if their continued presence sickens and weakens you.

It's also possible that the treasure thieves in your life could be co-workers. If they are petty thieves, you may just want to view them with a different set of lenses. Find a way to see through their actions, to the insecurity or pain that is below the surface so their actions affect you less. If they are committing grand larceny, that's a different story. Again, find your voice. Be diplomatic, fine, but don't be quiet. Follow the chain of command. And maybe the upper chain is the issue. If you can't wrap your head around their actions in a way that preserves your inner peace, and you don't have options to avoid them, then you've got some bigger decision making to do.

Negative people act like kryptonite. Choose accordingly. Once you realize how valuable your self esteem and peace are, the choices you need to make will come easier to you.

Where else does BS come from? When you turn on the television, you open the door to your inner psyche. I want to be clear here. You are *not* simply a casual observer. You're opening a loop. You are choosing to invite people, drama, and ideas into your inner world. Does what you watch wind you up or wind you down? Do you feel happier, more relaxed, and inspired? Or sad, nervous, and self conscious? This is completely in your power to recognize and choose. No one forces you to watch anything on television. And if they do, refer back a few paragraphs. Do you deliberately turn on the news? Do you do so in the morning, at the start of your day? Stop. Just stop. You set the tone for your entire day, and it's not the tone that serves you best.

You're most likely on social media (we'll talk about that next.) If something major is going on, you will hear about it. You don't need the news to keep you informed. Because the news will inform you of what's wrong with the world. The news will show you the worst in people. Hating hate doesn't make the situation better. This is not your most powerful point of focus. Here's an idea. Leave the television off. Start your day by writing one or ten things you are grateful for and putting them in a daily gratitude jar.

Will you tune into your favorite crime drama tonight? A scripted series about pain, fear, and bad people? And then go to bed after having invited that in? Break that habit. Let go of the need to see how next week will play out. Turn on a comedy or learn something instead. Or, shut the freaking thing off. Light a candle and read a book. Or journal. Or knit. Or color. Do anything that invites something better in and let's something creative out.

Perhaps the most powerful way you can unfollow the bullshit is via the most prevalent source of soul-sucking, confidence-crushing, fear-inducing garbage is with social media. Social media in and of itself isn't necessarily a bad thing. I love seeing what my cousins and their kids are up to. I love following smart people who post inspiring quotes and ideas. And I love sharing posts about pets up for adoption or inspiring quotes and ideas myself.

Get on the right loop. Unfollow the pages or people that don't make you feel better about yourself and your circumstances. It's as easy as a click. Clean house. Think of it as cleaning out your closet. Get rid of the shit that you don't love, so all that comes to you through your social media accounts is what you love, what makes you laugh, what fosters your creativity and sense of self worth. Search out new pages and people who inspire you, who help you see what is right about you and the world you live in.

Following the negativity, the people and pages that focus on our differences, is like leaving your treasure out in the open for pilfering. A little nugget here, a little nugget there and before you know it, you feel worthless. Shut that door.

A few years back, I had a follower of my Facebook page who was in a horrible state. I knew this because she changed her profile picture to words. I don't remember exactly what they were, but I knew this person was in pain and feeling dangerously low. I reached out to her and began a dialogue. I don't remember exactly what she was going through at the time. I do know she has a special needs son. Today, she doesn't just follow my page. We are Facebook friends. Her turn around has been miraculous. I'm not taking credit for it but I was witness to it. She changed her profile picture to something different. She very deliberately followed inspiring pages. I could see she did so because she regularly shared positive posts. I watched her transform. It was remarkable. Then I saw her post she was in a relationship. Then got engaged. And then married to a wonderful man who adores her. Her life may not be perfect, but she took deliberate action and chose to protect and invest in the treasure of her inner peace. She stepped into her alternate universe.

We live in the information age. We have more knowledge available to us in an instant than any time in previous history. This is fantastic and powerful in many ways. Our access to information is virtually unlimited. Your job is to become your own filter. The problem isn't access to information. The challenge is choosing what *not* to access. It's like putting on mental sunscreen so you don't get burned.

Going back to an earlier chapter, that negative narrative

inside your head is also something to address. Don't hate on it. Don't try to crush it. Engage with it, look for the positive intention behind it, and practice gently moving the dialogue in a better direction. Filter your own thoughts. Set a few alarms on your cell phone throughout the day that remind you to focus on the good. Right now I've got one set mid morning that says "You've got this," and another mid afternoon that says "You will always be provided for."

The more you deliberately clean house around you via the people, channels and pages, your internal dialogue will follow along. It has to.

It's not just what you expose yourself to. It's also your interpretation of what you see and the meaning you attach to it. It's the story you create as a result of what you see. When you see a post about dogs up for adoption, it could tug at your heart because they don't have a home. That could be the piece of the story you latch onto. Or you can feel gratitude for the people and organizations that help place them and the good social media is used for. You could learn of a natural disaster and feel saddened. Allow space for that. That's okay. Then look for and feel gratitude for how the best in humanity shows up when people are in need. Watch the kindness and generosity within us come to the surface as people open up their wallets and hearts and even sometimes risk their own lives to help each other.

As you unfollow the bullshit, you begin to follow the path of feeling right in your life, of stressing less and smiling more. You get out of the mud of stagnancy and powerless-ness and start moving toward the power of becoming the creator of the life you desire.

Unfollow the bullshit. Follow your bliss instead.

Beauty Regimen

Identify inspiring messages you need to keep in mind
to help you feel better about yourself and/or
achieve that which you desire.
Set at least two daily alarms in your phone
with these messages. Choose a ring tone that feels
good to you or a song that inspires you
to go along with it.

9

Grace, the Final Frontier

When people feel beautiful, they act in beautiful ways.

— Wayne Dyer

You understand now that your whole self and the sum of your experiences are uniquely yours and when brought together, have the capacity to create powerful change for you and generations to come. You've discovered that fighting against aspects of yourself weakens you and limits what you are capable of achieving. And that rather than seeing those aspects or experiences as flaws, bad luck, or unfortunate, you choose to integrate them in to who you are and how you show up in this world thereby unleashing powerful reserves of energy and wisdom. You redirect forces you previously applied to wishing away the reality of your past or trying to change the truth (and beauty) of who you are and use them to achieve the inner and outer conditions you desire. With renewed compassion for what is and by asking the right questions, you bring yourself closer to a sense of peace and clarity on how to create positive outcomes not in spite of, but as a direct result of your experiences.

Let's carry this concept a step forward. Or shall I say "outward"? How can we take what we've discussed so far and apply that to your impact on other people and humanity.

If judging aspects of ourselves and/or our individual experiences as negative or unfortunate and trying to ignore, feel anger or hatred toward them weakens us and limits our potential, could the same be said for how we perceive others?

How many times a day do we see a post on social media, pass a person at the mall, or see someone driving aggressively, and judge him or her negatively? Come on. We all do it. We shake our heads, curse under our breath or maybe even at the top of our lungs, wondering what's become of society. With one small interaction, often times not even involving a direct conversation, we determine him or her to be an asshole, stupid, lazy, or all of the above. Wrap that little judgment in a neat little summary and conclusion. Enter the weakness of separation. Exit the power of wholeness.

I'm not saying there aren't people out there making decisions that cause harm, to put it lightly. I get it. But do we empower ourselves and others by judging them? Does it work when we do it with ourselves? No. We've established that. So how will that same thinking create a better, more productive, and compassionate society? It can't.

"Be the change." said Gandhi. Three words. I'm writing a whole book to get this point across. He did it in three words. Now, you may be an activist at heart, someone who sees a need, rolls up her sleeves, and dives in to make a difference. That's awesome. We need people like you. I'm grateful for people like you. But this isn't the only way we alter the future course for the better. Just you coming to terms with the sum of you and your experiences will have a ripple effect of proportions greater than you can imagine. Know that. Rest assured, you will set in motion an infinite number of positive experiences, changes and outcomes for people you know and love and people whom you will never meet. No question. No need to be an activist to leave a trail of positive reactions in your wake.

So on one end of the spectrum of integrative possibilities, you have personal integration. On the other end of the spectrum, you have the person who chooses to become an activist for a cause and make a difference in that way. In between the two is a massive opportunity to "be the change." It's called today. It's called this moment. It's called every day life. Throughout your day and in every interaction you have with another person, you hold the power to seek to understand, to not dismiss, but to show compassion, to not judge, but to create a positive shift for another and you, and not perpetuate the very thing you wish didn't exist.

Hating hate doesn't diminish it. It magnifies it. Understand this. There is immense pain and fear behind the face of hate. If in your lifetime, you want to bring humanity closer together and increase peace, the only way to do that is to be the one who judges less and seeks more to understand and show compassion. If someone is acting angrily, what would happen if rather than walking away or matching their demeanor, you sincerely said "Hey, you okay? Anything I can do for you?" and then honest to God really *listened* to them?

Did you get wind of how the comedienne Sarah Silverman responded to a Twitter troll? A follower posted a one-word comment on a post of hers. It was the worst word you could use for a female. Sarah had three options in how to respond. One, she is highly intelligent and quick on her feet and is certainly capable of engaging in and winning a Twitter war. But she chose not to. Two, she could easily have deleted and blocked the guy. She chose not to. What did she choose? She clicked on his profile to learn more about him. Turns out the guy had major back issues and was in a lot of pain. He also lacked the insurance and resources to have surgery. She saw through his anger, intuitively knowing that behind that face of hatred, was another human being in pain and crying out for help. She decided to engage with him. Look it up. The conversation is amazing. The transformation in his demeanor from the beginning to the end of the conversation is remarkable. She ended up asking all of her followers who was in to help the guy. People stepped up. He got the help he needed.

Do you realize the magnitude of what she did by not judging and instead seeking to understand? She literally turned this man's life around. The comments from others that followed were amazing. Not only did she turn his life around, but she warmed the hearts of many others, inspired them to do the same and offered a renewed faith in the goodness of people . . . with one singular choice. This is the power we all possess.

In *Happy Bitch*, I talk about the "magical gaps." These are the moments of pause where your power lives. In between what stimulus comes at you and your response is a gap, an opening, a single point in time in which the future course and outcome is determined by *how you choose to respond*.

When in a dark room, you don't create light by pushing darkness out. You can't eliminate it. You can only turn on the light. The darkness disappears instantly when you do. We can apply this same principle to enacting positive change around us. In the presence of darkness, we can choose to be the light. Light is love, understanding, and compassion.

I've shared a simple story many times while speaking that I want to share here with you. It illustrates this point perfectly. I was in Target shopping one day. I had something to return and on my way to the service desk, I passed a register with a display of snacks and candy. I was hungry, so I grabbed two Kind bars and made my way to customer service with my return. I approached the counter, and the woman working there was clearly in a mood. She angrily tossed items into bins and wouldn't make eye contact with me. Everything about her body language said "Fuck off!"

Now, being honest, what are the typical thoughts you might have in response to this? "If she hates her job that much, she should look for another one. If people like me didn't shop here, she wouldn't have a job. She should be thankful she is employed." And on and on. I've thought every one of them. Keeping it real here. I could have put my figurative or literal hands on my hips and asked to speak to a supervisor. I had every right to. But this day, I chose otherwise and have countless times since then. I put on the lens of curiosity, of compassion, of seeking to understand with a desire to shift her energy and help lift her burdens. Clearly something was bothering her. How could I, someone returning a sweater, having never met her, leave her a little better off than before I interacted with her? You don't need to be famous or have a million followers to make a difference.

She turned my direction to process my return, still stern faced and not looking me in the eyes. I placed my fingertips on one of the two Kind bars and pushed it toward her. I said "Would you like this? It looks like you're having a bad day."

She stopped what she was doing, looked me right in the eyes and said "Are you kidding me? No. I'm not hungry, but you just completely made my day. I just came in to start my shift, and the person before me did not do their job, leaving all of this work to me. Thank you. I can't believe you just did that."

Come on! How hard was that? I didn't hate on her attitude, and believe me, she had one! I had an open mind. I chose not to judge her and looked to connect with her (read integrate,) and see how I might turn her in a better direction. This was a few years ago, and I remember it like it was this morning. It was such a seemingly simple gesture on my part. Yet look what it did for her. And what was the ripple effect? How do you think she greeted the next customer? How was she toward her family when she went home that night? How many times did she look for an opportunity to do the same for someone else since that day? How many times has she told this story to people in her circle who might be inspired to pay it forward?

I wrote about kindness in my first book. In fact I dedicated a whole chapter to it. I called it "The Perfect Drug." A kind and thoughtful gesture toward another person with zero expectation for anything in return is the fastest route to you feeling better about yourself. When you perform an act of kindness, your brain, the greatest pharmacy on planet earth, releases Serotonin. That's the same drug found in anti-depressants. And you can get as much as you want without a prescription or co-pay, in unlimited supply and without any negative side effects. On. Freaking. Demand.

Thoughtful gestures and acts of kindness are powerful, and yet there are times when all the situation calls for is someone to truly listen, to make another person feel understood. Seeking to understand is an act of compassion on its own. The other person will sense your genuineness and caring, and you will have created a bond, adding a thread of strength to this complicated weave of life.

When you answer the phone at work and a client or customer is short or rude, are you going to match him? Give it back because you have the right to? You could. Perhaps you have many times in the past. Or will you pause for a moment and ask a few questions attempting to genuinely understand why he is giving off that vibe? It's *unbelievable* how you can disarm someone by doing so.

The strong presence today of social media has many fantastic benefits. We can keep up with friends and family, share experiences and memories, and even be part of significant efforts to support a good cause. Yet it also lends itself to amplifying certain issues. Namely, comparison and a strong focus on our differences . . . whether that is in how much money we have, the color of our skin, or our political beliefs. The more we focus on and find issue with our differences, rather than respecting them and looking for what we share in common, the more we divide and weaken ourselves as a society. It's the macro-scale equivalent of how we fragment and weaken ourselves. Connect, don't compare.

I'm sure you've heard the term "Namaste." Do you know what it means? It essentially means "I honor the divine in each of us." In other words, where we are one, where we are connected. From the highest viewpoint possible, we are *all* connected.

Every cell in your body is a part of the greater whole that is you. Each is part of a system that works together to give you life. The same is true for each of us as an individual person who is part of humanity as a whole.

Maybe you already see the dynamics of life this way. Or perhaps this creates a new awareness of our connection to each other and your ability to influence others. If so, you may be thinking *Okay, this sounds plausible, but how? How do I develop the ability to see things this way?* It starts by turning on the curiosity with a genuine desire to understand. Then begin looking for what you share in common with another person. Keep going higher and higher until you find that point where we hold something in common. This is the highest vision and most powerful position you can take. It's where you bond with another person.

Do you love your family? They do too. Do you want the ones you love who are struggling to find peace? They do too. Do you want to feel good about yourself? So do they. Have you had some shit go down in your lifetime? So have they.

Do you want to be happy and know your life matters? They do too. I could go on, but you get the point.

We're not meant to go it alone. We are in this together. We are meant to be strong and healthy and contribute to the life and health of humanity as a whole. Strengthen bonds where you can and you strengthen yourself and your ability to find peace and manifest the experiences and feelings you desire. When you enrich the life of another, you have no choice but to enrich your own.

Having an open mind, looking for what's good in another person and seeking ways to help others is not only an outward act of compassion, it's an inward act of building self confidence. Looking for what you share in common with others and choosing to think, speak, and act *from that point* creates solidarity, strength, and power for you and the collective whole. As you integrate this manor of seeing others and choose your interactions carefully, you develop a sense of ease and grace about you. You move, think, and act grounded with a sense of connectedness, peace, and quiet confidence. And where confidence and peace reside, self doubt and fear cannot exist. As your self doubt and fear dissipate, you create the conditions and opportunity for the truth of who you are and your true beauty to emerge. I remind you of the analogy of turning on the light in a dark room. Stay mindful of your connection to and impact on the whole . . . not only within you, but around you as well.

I mentioned above and emphasized "from that point." I want to expand on this for a moment. When your actions will affect another individual, including as simple as a comment and the tone in which it's delivered, create the habit of asking

and being honest with yourself "What are my intentions?"
Any time the truth of the matter is you want to show you're
right and the other is wrong, return a jab (even if delivered
with a smile and passive-aggressive behavior,) or in any
manner leaving the other person pissed off, put in his or her
place, or shamed in any way, check in with yourself. You will
never advance the state of your own happiness when you
deliberately reduce another's. I'm not saying don't speak up
where you need to, but pause, be diplomatic and considerate
of how the other person will feel. By the way, shame is the
lowest of all human emotions. Please, please do your best not
to speak or act in a way that your intention is to make the
other person feel shameful.

With any decision, ask yourself "What is the outcome I
desire? Will what I'm about to do or say get me closer to or
further from what I want?" And again, this point is so
important. What you really want is not to make another
person feel bad. It's not going to help you. What you really
want is to feel good about yourself, happy, and confident.
You want to feel like a beautiful person.

There is one more area of impact on others I want you
to consider. You came here to bring forth something to this
world that no other person, dead, alive, or yet to be born,
could ever do. The purpose of your life is greater than
surviving. The purpose of your life is to gather everything
together, including all aspects of you, your experiences, your
natural talents and gifts, and with love in your heart, have the
courage to deliver that to the world. This could be as simple
as sitting with dogs at a shelter giving them love, committing
to be a teacher for children who need a heart-centered role

model, or writing books and becoming a world-renowned speaker who transforms the lives of millions. The volume of people (or animals) you impact is not the point. The point is to do you. If you've yet to gain clarity on what that is, follow your bliss. Your pain is the portal. Your bliss is the map once you step through.

Howard Thurman said it best. "Don't ask what the world needs. Ask what makes you come alive, and go do it. Because what the world needs is people who have come alive."

It is my hope this book has helped you do just that. Namaste.

Beauty Regimen

Perform an act of kindness today. Buy a stranger
a cup of coffee, send a text to a friend or relative telling her
how grateful you are to have her in
your life, or pick up a trinket or snack for a co-worker. Leave
it on her desk or in her workspace without her knowing.
Or whatever idea feels right to you.
(Check out *Share this Journal* on Amazon
which creates a documented chain of
random acts of kindness.)

Conclusion

Beauty begins the moment you decide to be yourself.

-Coco Chanel

Well my beautiful friend, the time has come for us to part ways . . . at least for now. But I will always be right here, in these pages, anytime you need me.

It is my deepest wish that I have brought to you all I could to help you feel whole again, to ease your fears, give you some peace, and help you well, be you again. I hope you've discovered some things about yourself and the power and wisdom within you to live your life to the fullest as well as influence, shape, and create your world in a way that allows you to sleep at night, cry if you need to, and laugh and giggle as often as you can.

If we ever meet, I will do my best to show up whole and true for you (and for myself) and invite you to do the same. If you're happy and excited, share that with me. I will join you in your joy. And if you feel sad or low, please know it's okay to not be okay with me. I won't judge you if you cry. I will hug you.

At the beginning of our time together, I mentioned that you need not concern yourself with being tough and strong. Not in the traditional sense anyway. I also asked you to trust me that there's nothing about you that is inadequate or flawed. Wounded maybe, but not flawed. I hope you now see that the path to feeling comfortable and confident in your own skin again is a whole lot more about healing you than changing or fixing you. It's less about effort and more about compassion and love.

I also told you that you would discover what it means to be powerful in a whole new way. While often viewed as a soft and even weak attribute of a female, our ability to feel and express compassion for ourselves and others is what I see as a source of immense power. And that it is in your welcoming of your wholeness and sharing that with the world, that you bring to and through you all the love you are capable of feeling and giving, the experiences that will bring you and others joy, the wisdom to know when to have faith and when to kick some ass, and finally come truly and fully alive. Can you imagine the ripple effect as each of us does this? I can already feel it.

I hope you're beginning to see a glimmer of what's possible for you. Maybe the spotlight is already shining bright on you and for you. In either case, please, don't ever give up on you. Discovering and living the life you are meant for, the one waiting and excited to greet you, is a bit like unlocking a unique code. You never know when you will try the next click and the door opens. Perhaps something in this book has done that for you, or at least gotten you a little closer.

I'm so happy to have shared this book with you. I hope you feel a sense of coming home, of a returning to what you once knew to be true . . . or *had* to be true, but you just couldn't seem to find your way. From all of me to all of you, I wish you peace, faith in yourself and life, and a bright future. You've got everything you need to step forth and bear witness to an entirely new world as it unfolds right before your eyes. It didn't come from this book. It's already within you. I just may have helped you see it.

For now my beautiful friend, I bid you adieu. Until we meet again.

About the Author

See paragraph two in the introduction.

www.KerylPesce.com
@kerylpesce

Other books by Keryl:

Happy Bitch
Pink Pretty Thoughts
Happiness Journal
Share this Journal (co-created with Amy Gopel)

Notes

1. Artie Wu, www.PresideMeditation.com.

2. Derek Rydall, (2015). *Emergence:* Atria Books/Beyond Words.

3. John Bowen *The Business Case for Being Really, Really Happy:* www.HuffingtonPost.com, December 6, 2017

4. Napolean Hill (1937). *Think and Grow Rich:* Sound Wisdom.

5. Masaru Emoto (2001). *The Hidden Messages in Water:* Beyond Words Publishing, Inc.

6. Pam Grout (2013). *E-Squared:* Hay House Insights.

Aha Moments

Aha Moments

Aha Moments

Aha Moments

Made in the
USA
Monee, IL